Stream Analytics with Microsoft Azure

Real-time data processing for quick insights using Azure
Stream Analytics

Anindita Basak
Krishna Venkataraman
Ryan Murphy
Manpreet Singh

BIRMINGHAM - MUMBAI

Stream Analytics with Microsoft Azure

Copyright © 2017 Packt Publishing

First published: November 2017

Production reference: 1201117

Published by Packt Publishing Ltd.
Livery Place
35 Livery Street
Birmingham
B3 2PB, UK.
ISBN 978-1-78839-590-8

www.packtpub.com

Credits

Authors
Anindita Basak
Krishna Venkataraman
Ryan Murphy
Manpreet Singh

Copy Editors
Tasneem Fatehi
Safis Editing

Reviewers
Ryan Murphy
Richard Iwasa
Vandana Saini

Project Coordinator
Manthan Patel

Commissioning Editor
Amey Varangaonkar

Proofreader
Safis Editing

Acquisition Editor
Tushar Gupta

Indexer
Pratik Shirodkar

Content Development Editor
Snehal Kolte

Graphics
Tania Dutta

Technical Editor
Sayli Nikalje

Production Coordinator
Shantanu Zagade

About the Authors

Anindita Basak is working as big data and cloud architect for a computer software giant and has been working with Microsoft Azure for the last 8+ years. She has worked with various teams of Microsoft as an FTE in the role of Azure Development Support Engineer, Pro-Direct Delivery Manager, Partner Technical Consultant. She has been a technical reviewer on five books by Packt on Azure HDInsight, SQL Server business intelligence, Hadoop development, smart learning with the Internet of Things (IoT), and decision science. Recently, she authored two video courses on Azure stream analytics by Packt. More details about her can be found on her LinkedIn profile at `https://www.linkedin.com/in/aninditabasak`.

I would like to dedicate this book to my dad, Ajit, my mom, Anjana, and my lovely brother, Aditya. Without your support, I couldn't have reached the goal of my life. Thanks for your patience and endless endurance.

Krishna Venkataraman is a cloud solution architect working with Microsoft. He has worked with a large public sector and Finserv customers around the world, building and deploying innovative solutions to solve their business challenges through technology and business process change. Currently, Krishna is helping Finserv and Telco with their cloud journey.

More details about his can be found on his LinkedIn profile: `https://www.linkedin.com/in/krishnavenk/v`.

I would like to thank my wife, Shailajha, our two angels and my extended family. Without their help and support, I won't have been able to complete this book. Thank you all the authors who collaborated with me to make this book a reality.

Ryan Murphy is a solution architect living in Saint Louis, Missouri, USA. He has been building and innovating with data for nearly 20 years, including extensive work in the gaming and agriculture industries. Currently, Ryan is helping some of the world's largest organizations modernize their business with data solutions powered by Microsoft Azure Cloud.

I would like to thank my wife, Meghan, and our three rapscallions (but especially Meghan) for tolerating my extended writing sessions. Thank you as well to the other fine authors for giving me the opportunity to collaborate and learn alongside a talented team.

Manpreet Singh is a consultant and author with extensive expertise in architecture, design, and implementation of Business Intelligence and big data analytics solutions. He is passionate about enabling businesses to derive valuable insights from their data.

Manpreet has been working on Microsoft technologies for more than 10 years, with a strong focus on Microsoft Business Intelligence Stack, SharePoint BI, and Microsoft's Big Data Analytics Platforms (Analytics Platform System and HDInsight). He also specializes in Mobile Business Intelligence solution development and has helped businesses deliver a consolidated view of their data to their mobile workforces.

Manpreet has coauthored books and technical articles on Microsoft technologies, focusing on the development of data analytics and visualization solutions with the Microsoft BI Stack and SharePoint. He holds a degree in computer science and engineering from Punjab University, India.

About the Reviewers

Ryan Murphy, is a solution architect living in Saint Louis, Missouri. He has been building and innovating with data for nearly twenty years, including extensive work in the gaming and agriculture industries. Currently, Ryan is helping some of the world's largest organizations modernize their business with data solutions powered by the Microsoft Azure Cloud.

Richard Iwasa, is currently working as a cloud solution architect with Microsoft and has been using Microsoft Azure since its inception. He has worked in IT and consulting for over 20 years across multiple industries, including transportation, resources, telecom, and financial services. Richard is passionate about using the cloud to solve his customers' business and technical challenges.

Vandana Saini (**Vinnie**), is an experienced data scientist with extensive experience in data analytics, consulting, information systems, and managing corporate clients for IT and financial institutions. She has worked with major Canadian banks and cloud service providers in the areas of artificial intelligence. Lately, she has been sharing her expertise as a cloud solution architect with Microsoft partners, augmenting AI capabilities towards transforming various industries.

Besides, she has delivered keynotes at various events for big data and analytics.

www.PacktPub.com

For support files and downloads related to your book, please visit www.PacktPub.com.

Did you know that Packt offers eBook versions of every book published, with PDF and ePub files available? You can upgrade to the eBook version at www.PacktPub.com and as a print book customer, you are entitled to a discount on the eBook copy. Get in touch with us at service@packtpub.com for more details.

At www.PacktPub.com, you can also read a collection of free technical articles, sign up for a range of free newsletters and receive exclusive discounts and offers on Packt books and eBooks.

https://www.packtpub.com/mapt

Get the most in-demand software skills with Mapt. Mapt gives you full access to all Packt books and video courses, as well as industry-leading tools to help you plan your personal development and advance your career.

Why subscribe?

- Fully searchable across every book published by Packt
- Copy and paste, print, and bookmark content
- On demand and accessible via a web browser

Customer Feedback

Thanks for purchasing this Packt book. At Packt, quality is at the heart of our editorial process. To help us improve, please leave us an honest review on this book's Amazon page at https://www.amazon.com/dp/1788395905.

If you'd like to join our team of regular reviewers, you can email us at customerreviews@packtpub.com. We award our regular reviewers with free eBooks and videos in exchange for their valuable feedback. Help us be relentless in improving our products!

Table of Contents

Preface

In this book, guidance will be provided for data architecture professionals, cloud architects, big data developers, and data scientists who would like to grab an end-to-end understanding of real-time complex streaming architecture. It's a comprehensive guidance on developing real-time event processing with Azure Stream Analysis.

And it's an implementation guidance for interactive data processing in fields such as the **Internet of Things** (**IoT**), social media, sensor data processing with BI, integration of streaming analytics with machine learning, and so on.

What this book covers

Chapter 1, *Introducing Stream Processing and Real-Time Insights*, describes a paradigm shift that is underway in data processing, from a legacy of handling static data in batches to handling continuously moving data in streams. We explore the fundamental architectural concepts of stream processing as well as its benefits in Real-Time Insights.

Chapter 2, *Introducing Azure Stream Analytics and Key Advantages*, introduces Microsoft's Azure Stream Analytics, a real-time analytics service built for the stream processing era. We walk through a basic Stream Analytics job configuration and then discuss its key features that drive down the total cost of ownership of streaming solutions.

Chapter 3, *Designing Real-Time Streaming Pipeline*, discusses the components of stream processing pipelines and how they differ from traditional batch pipelines, including temporal concepts such as windowing, hot and cold paths of data movement, and others. To see how streaming design concepts can be applied to a technical architecture, we then look at the canonical Azure streaming pipeline from data generation to intelligent action.

Chapter 4, *Developing Real-Time Event Processing with Azure Streaming*, covers various tools for provisioning a Stream Analytics job. The integration steps of job input and output are demonstrated.

Chapter 5, *Building Using Stream Analytics Query Language*, explores the SQL-like query language used in Azure Stream Analytics to run transformations and computations on streaming data. Common and complex stream processing requirements can be met with straightforward queries.

Chapter 6, *How to achieve Seamless Scalability with Automation*, covers deploying at the enterprise-grade with features and patterns for scaling and deployment automation. After demonstrating automated deployment using **Azure Resource Manager** (**ARM**), we explore vertical and horizontal partitioning and scaling in Stream Analytics to increase job capacity and performance.

Chapter 7, *Integration of Microsoft Business Intelligence and Big Data*, discusses the modern data solution architectures Lambda and Kappa, how to use Stream Analytics to comport with these architectures, and compare it with a popular alternative, HDInsight Storm. We then walk through a sample pipeline, implementing a real-time dashboard based on the Power BI output connector for Stream Analytics.

Chapter 8, *Designing and Managing Stream Analytics Jobs*, explore solutions to complex challenges of managing streaming jobs, starting with the common need to integrate streams with static data. We then discuss integration with Azure Data Lake Store and Cosmos DB as examples of Azure services whose native integration with Stream Analytics offers unique opportunities to enhance streaming pipelines.

Chapter 9, *Optimizing Intelligence in Azure Streaming*, discusses building intelligence directly into Stream Analytics jobs so that extensible functions and machine learning calls execute in real time as data moves. We cover integration with the Azure Machine Learning service and implementing user-defined JavaScript functions in Stream Analytics queries. Finally, we walk through using the Azure .NET SDK to enhance job management.

Chapter 10, *Understanding Stream Analytics Job Monitoring*, looks into ongoing maintenance and job management. We discuss and demonstrate the job metrics, diagram, and logging features offered by Stream Analytics, as well as service health dashboarding and alerting.

Chapter 11, *Use Cases of Real-World Data Streaming Architectures*, is an end-to-end real-life use case demonstration using the Azure IoT suite with Stream Analytics with implementation steps as PoC for Social Sentiment Analytics, IoT Remote Monitoring telemetry solution, connected factory, and PoC on fraud detection Analytics from the telecom industry.

What you need for this book

1. A valid Azure subscription
2. Visual Studio 2017/2015
3. Azure SDK 2.7.1 or higher
4. Azure Storage Explorer
5. A Power BI Office 365 account
6. Python SDK 2.7 (x64) bit and packages

Who this book is for

If you are looking for a resource that teaches you how to process continuous streams of data in real time, this book is what you need. A basic understanding of the concepts of analytics is all you need to get started with this book.

Conventions

In this book, you will find a number of text styles that distinguish between different kinds of information. Here are some examples of these styles and an explanation of their meaning.

Code words in text, database table names, folder names, filenames, file extensions, pathnames, dummy URLs, user input, and Twitter handles are shown as follows: "Once the ASA job is created, in the `Solution Explorer`, the job topology folder structure could be viewed as Inputs (job input), Outputs (job output), `JobConfig.json`, `Script.asaql` (Stream Analytics Query file), Azure Functions (optional), and so on."

A block of code is set as follows:

```
Select input.vin, BlobSource.Model, input.timestamp,
input.outsideTemperature,
input.engineTemperature, input.speed, input.fuel, input.engineoil,
input.tirepressure, input.odometer, input.city,
input.accelerator_pedal_position,
input.parking_brake_status,
input.headlamp_status, input.brake_pedal_status,
input.transmission_gear_position, input.ignition_status,
input.windshield_wiper_status, input.abs into output from input join
BlobSource
on input.vin = BlobSource.VI
```

New terms and **important words** are shown in bold.

Words that you see on the screen, for example, in menus or dialogue boxes, appear in the text like this: "To run the Stream Analytics job query locally, first select **Add Local Input** by right-clicking on the ASA project in VS Solution Explorer, and choose to **Add Local Input.**"

 Warnings or important notes appear like this.

 Tips and tricks appear like this.

Reader feedback

Feedback from our readers is always welcome. Let us know what you think about this book-what you liked or disliked. Reader feedback is important for us as it helps us develop titles that you will really get the most out of. To send us general feedback, simply email feedback@packtpub.com, and mention the book's title on the subject of your message. If there is a topic that you have expertise in and you are interested in either writing or contributing to a book, see our author guide at www.packtpub.com/authors.

Customer support

Now that you are the proud owner of a Packt book, we have a number of things to help you to get the most from your purchase.

Downloading the example code

You can download the example code files for this book from your account at http://www.packtpub.com. If you purchased this book elsewhere, you can visit http://www.packtpub.com/support and register to have the files emailed directly to you. You can download the code files by following these steps:

1. Log in or register to our website using your email address and password.
2. Hover the mouse pointer on the **SUPPORT** tab at the top.
3. Click on **Code Downloads & Errata**.

4. Enter the name of the book in the **Search** box.
5. Select the book for which you're looking to download the code files.
6. Choose from the drop-down menu where you purchased this book from.
7. Click on **Code Download**.

Once the file is downloaded, please make sure that you unzip or extract the folder using the latest version of:

- WinRAR / 7-Zip for Windows
- Zipeg / iZip / UnRarX for Mac
- 7-Zip / PeaZip for Linux

The code bundle for the book is also hosted on GitHub at `https://github.com/PacktPublishing/Stream-Analytics-with-Microsoft-Azure`. We also have other code bundles from our rich catalogue of books and videos available at `https://github.com/PacktPublishing/`. Check them out!

Downloading the color images of this book

We also provide you with a PDF file that has color images of the screenshots/diagrams used in this book. The color images will help you better understand the changes in the output. You can download this file from `https://www.packtpub.com/sites/default/files/downloads/StreamAnalyticswithMicrosoftAzure_ColorImages.pdf`.

Errata

Although we have taken every care to ensure the accuracy of our content, mistakes do happen. If you find a mistake in one of our books-maybe a mistake in the text or the code-we would be grateful if you could report this to us. By doing so, you can save other readers from frustration and help us improve subsequent versions of this book. If you find any errata, please report them by visiting `http://www.packtpub.com/submit-errata`, selecting your book, clicking on the **Errata Submission Form** link, and entering the details of your errata. Once your errata are verified, your submission will be accepted and the errata will be uploaded to our website or added to any list of existing errata under the Errata section of that title. To view the previously submitted errata, go to `https://www.packtpub.com/books/content/support` and enter the name of the book in the search field. The required information will appear under the **Errata** section.

Piracy

Piracy of copyrighted material on the internet is an ongoing problem across all media. At Packt, we take the protection of our copyright and licenses very seriously. If you come across any illegal copies of our works in any form on the internet, please provide us with the location address or website name immediately so that we can pursue a remedy. Please contact us at `copyright@packtpub.com` with a link to the suspected pirated material. We appreciate your help in protecting our authors and our ability to bring you valuable content.

Questions

If you have a problem with any aspect of this book, you can contact us at `questions@packtpub.com`, and we will do our best to address the problem.

1

Introducing Stream Processing and Real-Time Insights

The popularity of stream data platforms is increasing significantly in recent times. Due to the requirement of real-time access to information. Enterprises are transitioning parts of their data infrastructure to a streaming paradigm due to changing business needs. The streaming model presents a significant shift by moving from point queries against stationary data to a standing temporal query that consumes moving data. Fundamentally, we enable insight on the data before it is stored in the analytics repository. This introduces a new paradigm in thinking. Before going deep into stream processing, we have to cover a couple of key basic concepts related to events and stream. In this chapter, we'll explore the basics of the following points:

- Publish/Subscribe (Pub/Sub)
- Stream processing
- Real-Time Insights

The core theme of this book is the Azure Streaming Service. Before diving deeper into Azure Streaming Service, we should take a moment to consider why we need stream processing, or Real-Time Insights, and why it is a tool worth adding to your repertoire.

Understanding stream processing

So what is stream processing and why is it important? In traditional data processing, data is typically processed in batch mode. The data will be dealt with on a regular schedule. One fundamental challenge with conventional data processing is it's inherently reactive because it focuses on ageing information. Stream processing, on the other hand, processes data as it flows through in real time.

The following are some of the highlights of why stream processing is critical:

- **Response time is critical**:
    - Reducing decision latency can unlock business value
    - Need to ask questions about data in motion
    - Can't wait for data to get to rest before running computation

- **Actions by human actors**:
    - See and seize insights
    - Live visualization
    - Alerts and alarms
    - Dynamic aggregation

- **Machine-to-machine interactions**:
    - Data movement with enrichment
    - Kick-off workflows for automation

Before one goes into stream analytics, it is essential to understand the core basics around events and different models of publishing and consuming events. Let's get more familiar with queues, Pub/Sub, and events, which will surely help you understand the later chapters better. In the following sections, we will explore queues, Pub/Sub, and events.

Understanding queues, Pub/Sub, and events

In this section, we will review two key concepts—queues and Publish/Subscribe models, followed by event-based messaging models.

Queues

A queue implements a one-way communication, where the sender places a message on the queue and a receiver will collect the message asynchronously. Features such as dead letter queues, paired namespaces, active/passive replication, and auto-forwarding to a chain queue that's part of the same name provide the rich feature set for message flowing between an application and providing a highly available solution.

A queue consists of three key elements:

- Sender: Sends the message to the receiver through a durable entity.
- Durable entity: Stores the received durable message and offers persistence. The messages are stored until they are collected by the receiver.
- Receiver: The final recipient of the message.

The key advantages of a queue are as follows:

- Queues operate on the principle of **first in**, **first out** (**FIFO**): For example, consider a simple queue where, at one end, you put messages, and on the other end you will receive them in the same respective order. For example, service bus queue implements the FIFO pattern.
- Point-to-point: The fundamental concept of Queues is, they are point-to-point messaging; even though there may be multiple senders of messages, there is only one receiver of the messages.
- Asynchronous communication: This implies that endpoint addresses are connected directly. A static structure may exist where senders and receivers communicate through named channels. Asynchronous communication helps with building decoupled architecture and allows higher resilience to add and process messages when either the publisher or consumer of messages has downtime.
- Security: Due to the mutual knowledge of senders and receivers from the security point of view, senders know where the data will land, and it's easier to enforce security policies.

The following figure illustrates the preceding concept:

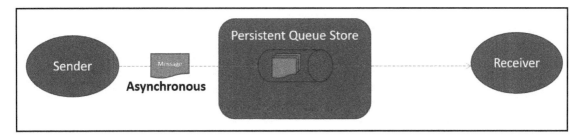

Publish and Subscribe model

Publish/Subscribe is a communication paradigm for a large-scale system. It enables loose coupling between mutually anonymous components and supports many-to-many communication.

The core concept of the Publish/Subscribe model is very simple. A Publisher publishes information on some topic, and anyone that is interested in the information will be able to find that information at the same time, simply by subscribing to that information. Well known example of this pattern is News Feeds and end user that are interested can subscribe to the type of news feeds they like to listen. Let's review key components in the Publish/Subscribe paradigm:

- Publisher (message sender):
    - Middleware connects the Publish/Subscribe middleware to communicate
    - Publishers produce events without any dependence on subscribers
    - Publishers advertise the events they are prepared to publish
    - The publisher announces an event without having any understanding of the potential subscriber
- Topic:
    - The topic is conceptually similar to the queue, but the topic can have a copy of a given message that is forwarded to multiple subscriptions
    - Topics and subscriptions provide a one-to-many form of communication-based on the Publish/Subscribe pattern
- Subscriber (receiver):
    - Subscribers register their interest in receiving events through a subscription that the middleware handles
    - The subscriber can subscribe and unsubscribe to events
    - The subscriber has to express interest in one or more events and only receive events related to their interest, without any knowledge of which publishers can provide that given event
- Subscription:
    - Provided once the event is received and a subscriber consumes it, the same event cannot be replaced, and new subscribers will not see the event to eliminate duplicate processing of events

- Subscription is similar to a virtual queue that receives copies of the message that were sent to the topic; you can optionally include filter rules for a topic on a per-subscription basis, which allows you to filter messages as illustrated:

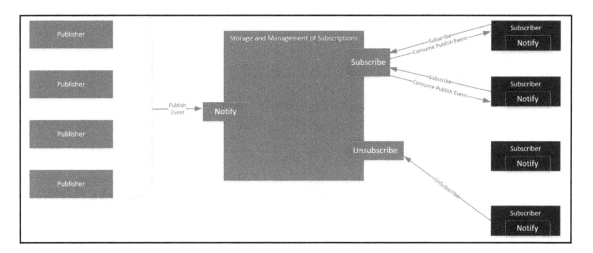

Key benefits of the Pub/Sub model are as follows:

- Decoupling (loose coupling): Space, time, synchronization decoupling:
  - Space: The publisher and subscriber don't need to know each other either by name or IP address, for instance.
  - Time: The publisher and subscriber don't need to run at the same time.
  - Synchronization: Operations can continue at both ends of the spectrum (publish and receiving).
- Highly parallel:
  - The model is highly parallel in that subscribers can process events and, at the same time, the publisher can keep publishing events.

- Scalability:
    - Due to the decoupling nature and parallel nature of the model, the Pub/Sub model is highly scalable.
    - To achieve higher velocity, events can cache and smarter routing to the subscriber can be configured to scale.
    - The key challenge with the Pub/Sub model is scaling to millions of publishers and subscribers.

In addition to the preceding, there are two key challenges with the Pub/Sub model:

- No guarantee of message delivery because of the decoupled nature of the model
- For applications that totally depend on guaranteed message delivery, the queue-based model will not fit

Real-world implementations of the Publish/Subscribe model

TIBCO is one of the pioneers that preached the Publish/Subscriber model during the time of centralized batch processing. The TIBCO approach changed the paradigm on the stock trading floor.

RSS Feeds use the Pub/Sub model; you subscribe to an RSS feed, to one or more forums on a discussions platform, or follow someone on Twitter--in each case, there is one publisher and multiple subscribers involved.

Companies like IBM build protocols like **Message Queue Telemetry Transport (MQTT)**. Some example of products that are built on the Pub/Sub model:

- IBM MQ is one of the early deployers of the Pub/Sub model
- Websphere
- Wormhole Pub/Sub system from Facebook
- Google Cloud Pub/Sub

In the next section, we will look how Azure implements queues and Pub/Sub models.

Azure implementation of queues and Publish/Subscribe models

Azure supports two types of queuing mechanism:

- Storage queues
- Service bus queues

Storage queues are part of the Azure storage infrastructure and offer a simple REST-based GET/PUT/PEEK interface. This does provide a reliable persistent messaging within and between the services.

Service bus queues are part of the enterprise offering of the Azure messaging infrastructure. As a part of the offering, it includes queues, Pub/Sub, and advanced integration patterns.

Both of these queuing technologies exist in parallel, to cater different type of use cases. Storage queues were first offered as a service to exist on top of the Azure storage service. Service bus queues came after storage queues and support wider use cases and scenarios. For example, if your components span multiple communication protocols, data contracts, trust domains, and network environments Azure Service Bus queues is the ideal solution.

There are a couple of key technical differences between Azure Storage queues and Azure Service Bus queues.

You should consider Azure Storage queues when:

1. Your queue size requires over 80 GB and messages will have a lifetime of shorter than seven days.
2. You are building on Azure worker roles and you want to preserve messages between worker roles crashes.
3. Server-side logs are required for all transactions executed against your queues.

You should consider Azure Service Bus queues:

1. When you want to be guaranteed FIFO ordered delivery.
2. When your solution requires duplicate detection.
3. When your (**Time to live** (**TTL**)) can exceed more than seven days and your message sizes are greater than 80 GB.

If you would like to understand the detailed differences between Azure Storage queues versus Azure Service Bus queues, visit `https://docs.microsoft.com/en-us/azure/ service-bus-messaging/service-bus-azure-and-service-bus-queues-compared- contrasted`.

Azure Service Bus messaging is an implementation message queuing concept implemented in the Microsoft Azure as a **Platform as a Service** (**PaaS**) offering. All Azure PaaS services are built with high resiliency and high availability.

In this section, we briefly reviewed Azure implements queues and Pub/Sub models. Since the goal of this book is Stream event processing, we will explore deeper into Azure Events in the next section.

What is an event?

An event is made of two parts, the event header, and the event body. The event header will have a name, the timestamp of the event, and type of event. The event body will have details of the event.

Events can be triggered by the business process or by many different types of activities.

Event streaming

Events are written to a common log. One of the key characteristics of event streaming is that they are strictly ordered (within a partition) and durable. One key difference between Azure Service Bus and events is that the clients don't subscribe to the stream. The client has the flexibility to read from any part of the stream and this opens multiple possibilities.

One major advantage is that a client can read from any part of the stream and the client is solely responsible for advancing their position in the stream. This enables the client to join at any given time and to replay events.

Event correlation

Event correlation is the process of trying to identify the cause of a situation or condition when massive amounts of data points (potentially related to the situation) exist.

Azure implementation of event processing

If you require receiving and processing millions of events per second, Azure Event Hub is the ideal solution. Typical use cases include tracking and monitoring telemetry collected from an industrial machine, mobile devices, and connected vehicles. For example, in-game events capture in-console applications.

Event Hubs work with low latency and at a massive scale, and serves as the on-ramp for big data:

The following screenshot is a canonical implementation of event processing on Azure:

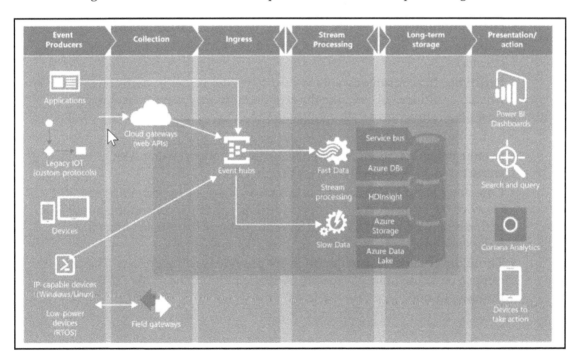

The Advanced Message Queuing Protocol 1.0 is a standardized framing and transfer protocol for asynchronously, securely, and reliably transferring messages between two parties. It is the primary protocol for Azure Service Bus Messaging and Azure Event Hubs. Both services also support HTTPS. The proprietary SBMP protocol that is also supported is being phased out in favor of AMQP.

AMQP 1.0 is the result of broad industry collaboration that brought together middleware vendors, such as Microsoft and Red Hat, with many messaging middleware users such as JP Morgan Chase representing the financial services industry. The technical standardization forum for the **Advanced Message Queuing Protocol** (**AMQP**) protocol and extension specifications is OASIS, and it has achieved formal approval as an international standard as ISO/IEC 19494.

Architectural components of Event Hubs

Event Hubs contain the following key elements:

- **Event producers/publishers**: The event can be published via AMQP or HTTPS.
- **Capture**: Azure Storage Blob item is used as a data storage repository for the events.
- **Partitions**: If a consumer wants to read a specific subset or partition of the event stream, partitions will provide the required options for the consumer.
- **SAS tokens**: Identity and authentication for the event publisher are provided by SAS tokens.
- **Event consumers** (receiver): Event consumers connect using AMQP 1.0. Any entity can read event data from an Event Hub.
- **Consumer groups**: Consumer groups provide a scale by providing separate views of the event stream. This provides each multiple consuming application with a separate view of the event stream, enabling those consumers to act independently.
- **Throughput units**: A throughput event provides scaling options. The customer can pre-purchase units of capacity. A single partition has a max scale of one throughput unit.

Azure Service Bus works on the competing consumer pattern. In the competing consumer pattern scenario, multiple consumers will process the messages as illustrated in the image shown as following.

These increases improve scalability and availability, on the same note, this pattern is useful for asynchronous message processing:

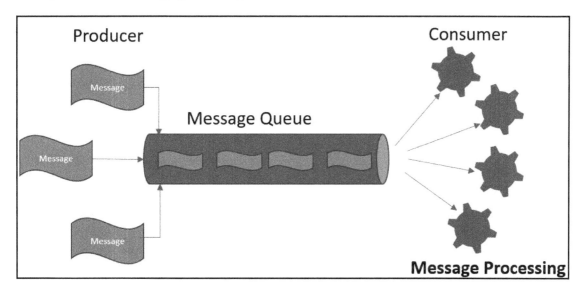

Event Hubs, on the other hand, work on the concept of partitions. Event Hub is composed of multiple partitions that will receive messages from publishers. As the volume of messages increase the number of partitions can be increased to handle the additional load.

Having partitions will increase the capacity to handle more messages and also have high throughput:

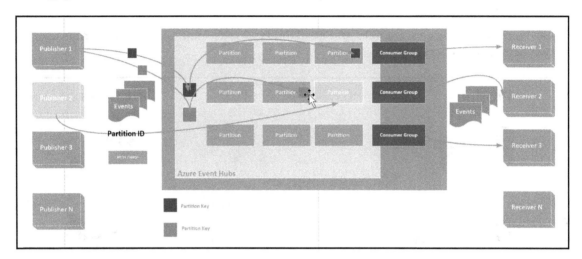

In summary, real-time streaming is all around us, be it a simple thermostat, your car telemetry, household electric meter data. Data is constantly streamed without anyone realizing it. For instance, when you are driving a car, the onboard computer is constantly doing the calculation on some telemetry data on the fly.

The final decision maker when it comes to the car is the driver that's in the driving seat. The same may not be true in other scenarios with modern day collision avoidance systems. If the onboard computer has enough data points that the car will collide with the car in front, it will decide to slow you down. That's where the real-time decision making comes into play.

The key objective of this book is to get you started on a very strong basis with event processing using Azure; as a reader, you can go on to do bigger and better things using this technology.

Before we dive further into this broad topic, let's see some of the core basics you need to know to get started.

An event-driven architecture can involve building a Publish and Subscribe, Event streaming model and a processing system:

- Publish/Subscribe: The underlying message infrastructure keeps track of subscriptions. Each subscriber will receive an event when it gets published.
  - After the event is received, it cannot be replayed and new subscribers cannot see the event. In other words, you get only one opportunity to process the message. There is no way to go back to message to re-process or retry.
- Event streaming: In event streaming, clients are independent of the event producers, and they read from a common logging system.
  - The client can read from any part of the system and they are responsible for advancing their posting in the stream.
  - It also gives them the flexibility to join at any time and replay events as they want. One key feature set of event streaming is that, in a given partition, they are sequentially ordered and durable.
- If you look at message or event data they are simply data with a timestamp. This data need be processed by applying business logic or rule to derive or create an outcome. There are 3 well-known processing systems:
  - Simple event processing
  - Event stream processing
  - Complex event processing

Simple event processing

An event immediately triggers into action in the consumer. For instance, you can use Azure Functions that can execute when it receives a message on the Service Bus topic.

Simple event processing (SEP) is used whenever you need to handle events in a simple way. There are not many differences between the events, the system will just process all of them.

In simple event processing, multiple single events will land into the processing engine. The events will be filtered, transformed, split, and routed. A classic example could be URL matching in a web server. Let's say you have a shopping portal and users can select different products, or click on different or the same products. In that instance, the web server will route the request, or the web server filters the request based on the URL it receives from the interactions and routes it accordingly.

The key characteristic of simple event processing is that a single event is processed without looking at other events. Events are processed at a time.

The following are the stages of the SEP:

- **Filter**: Filtering the event stream for a specific type of event
- **Transform**: Transforming events schema from one form to another
- **Enrich**: Augmenting the event payload with additional data
- **Split**: Splitting the events into multiple events and processing them
- **Route**: Moving the event from one channel or stream to another

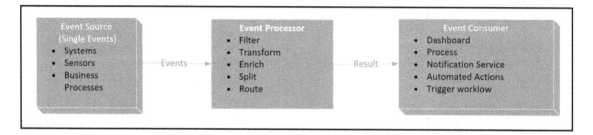

Event stream processing

Continuous streams of data are processed in real time by applying a series of operations (stream processors) on each data point. The **event stream processors** (**ESP**) will act to process or transform the stream of data.

For example, one can use data streaming platforms, such as Azure IoT Hub or Apache Kafka, to act as a pipeline to ingest events and feed them to stream processors as showcased in the following illustration. Depending on the scale and complexity, there will be more than one stream processor to work on various subsystems of that given application. This approach is a good fit for clickstream analytics, IoT and device telemetry, credit fraud detection:

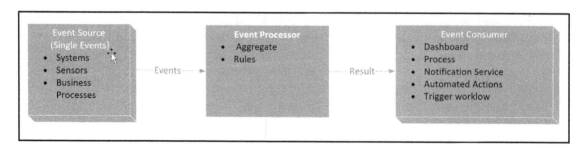

Complex event processing

Forrester defines a CEP platform as, a software infrastructure that can detect patterns of events (and expected events that didn't occur) by filtering, correlating, contextualizing, and analyzing data captured from disparate live data sources to respond as defined using the platform's development tools.

Complex event processing (**CEP**) is a subset of event stream processing. CEP enables you to gain insights from large volumes of data in near real-time by monitoring, analyzing, and acting on data while it is in motion. Data is typically generated by business or system events such as placing an order or adding a message to a queue. CEP is the continuous monitoring and processing of events from multiple sources on a near real-time basis. Since CEP enables the analysis of data in real-time, it lends itself to predictive scenarios to enable more proactive decisions.

Typical scenarios may include:

- Monitoring the effectiveness of key performance indicators (KPIs) by using data from event streams
- Monitoring the health and availability of servers, networks and service level threshold compliance
- Fraud detection
- Stock ticker analysis—taking action when certain events occur or price points are achieved
- Performance history—predicting spikes
- Buying patterns (what product/pricing combinations are most popular)

The concept behind CEP is the aggregation of information over a time window or looking for a pattern and generating a notification when the aggregation of data or pattern breaches a defined condition. The emphasis is placed on detection of the event.

CEP has its origins in the stock market and, because of this fact, it is tuned for low latency and often responds in a few milliseconds or sub-milliseconds. Some of the events can be ignored without impact.

Internet of things (**IoT**) applications are very good to use cases for CEP since they are time series data, auto-correlated. IoT use cases are usually complex and they go beyond aggregation and calculation of data. These types of cases need complex operations such as time windows and temporal query patterns. Due to the availability of temporal operators, it's easy to process time series data efficiently. The following figure illustrations showcase CEP Flow:

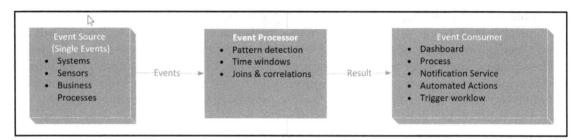

Summary

In this chapter, we covered Publish/Subscribe, events, and complex event processing.

In the following chapters, we will look at hands-on labs and also more details into how these features can be implemented in Azure.

2
Introducing Azure Stream Analytics and Key Advantages

Microsoft provides a portfolio of data platform products that includes large volume/scale storage, processing, and orchestration of events. One key advantage offered by these services is that customers can deploy a combination of services and create new offerings that are very specific to their needs.

In this chapter, we will introduce Azure Stream Analytics, get into the configuration, look at the advantages of the Stream Analytics platform and focus on how it will enhance developer productivity and reduce or improve the **Total Cost of Ownership** (**TCO**) of building and maintaining a scaling streaming solution.

Let's start working on the material.

Services offered by Microsoft

The following is a very well-known classification of the different type of services offered by Microsoft for on-premises and the cloud. Microsoft Azure provides a full spectrum of services starting with **Infrastructure as a Service (IaaS)**, followed by **Platform as a Service (PaaS)** and **Software as a Service (SaaS)** models such as Dynamics CRM, Office 365, and so on:

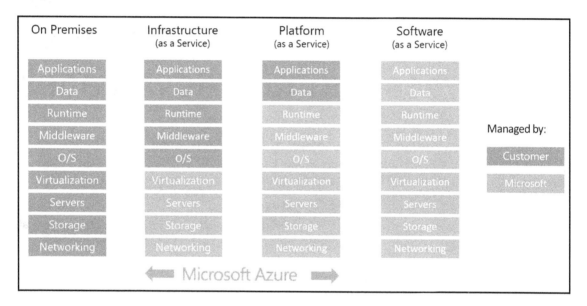

Service classification model

With IaaS, customers can deploy a virtual machine of their choice without the complexity of buying and managing their own hardware/software; they can quickly scale up and down with demand and pay only for what they use. This will reduce operational expenses of hosting and managing infrastructure.

Azure provides a vast range of PaaS services such as web apps, logic apps, media apps, API apps, mobile apps, Azure Stream Analytics, Azure HDInsight, and Azure Redis Cache. PaaS services like **PowerApps** are targeted at business users to create simple mobile apps and business workflows, without requiring any knowledge of a programming language. PaaS is an exciting model, where Microsoft will take care of all the core infrastructure to the point where the application and data become the responsibility of the customer.

One most common question is whether a customer should choose between IaaS versus PaaS. The comparison itself forms a very vast subject. Let's focus on the key point of the trade-off between them. One key trade-off is between speed and control within the cloud environment. PaaS-based services offer less control over infrastructure components but offer high velocity in terms of speed of deployment and easier maintenance (example: automated patching of the guest OS). On the other hand, the traditional IaaS-based deployment model is build using a **virtual machine** (**VM**), as they offer the most control in the cloud environment.

Azure provides customers with multiple entry points that give them different agility, control, and flexibility in their development and production environment. What that means for customers is that they have more choices in building their application and different entry points along a control-speed continuum. Our primary focus for this book is PaaS based streaming solution based on Azure Stream Analytics. Let's go deep into the topic in the next section.

Introduction to Azure Stream Analytics

Microsoft Azure Stream Analytics falls into the category of PaaS services where the customers don't need to manage the underlying infrastructure. However, they are still responsible and manage an application that builds on the top of PaaS service and more importantly the customer data.

Azure Stream Analytics is a fully managed server-less PaaS service that is built for real-time analytics computations on streaming data. The service can consume from a multitude of sources. Azure will take care of the hosting, scaling, and management of the underlying hardware and software ecosystem. The following are some of the examples of different use cases for Azure Stream Analytics.

When we are designing the solution that involves streaming data, in almost every case, Azure Stream Analytics will be part of a larger solution that the customer was trying to deploy. This can be real-time dashboarding for monitoring purposes or real-time monitoring of IT infrastructure equipment, preventive maintenance (auto-manufacturing, vending machines, and so on), and fraud detection. This means that the streaming solution needs to be thoughtful about providing out-of-the-box integration with a whole plethora of services that could help build a solution in a relatively quick fashion.

Let's review a usage pattern for Azure Stream Analytics using a canonical model:

Azure Stream Analytics using a canonical model

We can see devices and applications that generate data on the left in the preceding illustration that can connect directly or through cloud gateways to your stream ingest sources. Azure Stream Analytics can pick up the data from these ingest sources, augment it with reference data, run necessary analytics, gather insights and push them downstream for action. You can trigger business processes, write the data to a database or directly view the anomalies on a dashboard.

In the previous canonical pattern, the number of streaming ingest technologies are used; let's review them in the following section:

- **Event Hub**: Global scale event ingestion system, where one can publish events from millions of sensors and applications. This will guarantee that as soon as an event comes in here, a subscriber can pick that event up within a few milliseconds. You can have one or more subscriber as well depending on your business requirements. A typical use case for an Event Hub is real-time financial fraud detection and social media sentiment analytics.

- **IoT Hub**: IoT Hub is very similar to Event Hub but takes the concept a lot further forward—in that you can take bidirectional actions. It will not only ingest data from sensors in real time but can also send commands back to them. It also enables you to do things like device management. Enabling fundamental aspects such as security is a primary need for IoT built with it.
- **Azure Blob:** Azure Blob is a massively scalable object storage for unstructured data, and is accessible through HTTP or HTTPS. Blob storage can expose data publicly to the world or store application data privately.
- **Reference Data:** This is auxiliary data that is either static or that changes slowly. Reference data can be used to enrich incoming data to perform correlation and lookups.

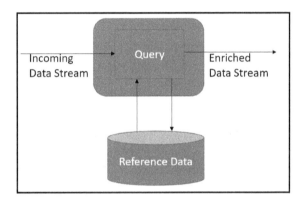

Using reference data in a streaming solution

On the ingress side, with a few clicks, you can connect to Event Hub, IOT Hub, or Blob storage. The Streaming data can be enriched with Reference data in the Blob store.

Data from the ingress process will be consumed by the Azure Stream Analytics service; we can call **machine learning** (**ML**) for event scoring in real time. The data can be egressed to live Dashboarding to Power BI, or could also push data back to Event Hub from where dashboards and reports can pick it up.

The following is a summary of the ingress, egress, and archiving options:

- Ingress choices:
    - Event Hub
    - IoT Hub
    - Blob storage
- Egress choices:
    - Live Dashboards:
        - Power BI
    - Event Hub
- Driving workflows:
    - Event Hubs
    - Service Bus
- Archiving and post analysis:
    - Blob storage
    - Document DB
    - Data Lake
    - SQL Server
    - Table storage
    - Azure Functions

One key point to note is there the number of customers who push data from Stream Analytics processing (egress point) to Event Hub and then add Azure website-as hosted solutions into their own custom dashboard. One can drive workflows by pushing the events to Azure Service Bus and Power BI.

For example, a customer can build IoT support solutions to detect an anomaly in connected appliances and pushing the result into Azure Service Bus. A worker role can run as a daemon to pull the messages and create support tickets using Dynamics CRM API. Then use Power BI on the ticket can be archived for post analysis. This solution eliminates the need for the customer to log a ticket, but the system will automatically do it based on predefined anomaly thresholds. This is just one sample of real-time connected solution.

There are a number of use cases that don't even involve real-time alerts. You can also use it to aggregate data, filter data, and store it in Blob storage, **Azure Data Lake** (**ADL**), Document DB, SQL, and then run U-SQL **Azure Data Lake Analytics** (**ADLA**), HDInsight, or even call ML models for things like predictive maintenance.

Configuration of Azure Stream Analytics

Azure Stream Analytics (**ASA**) is a fully managed, cost-effective real-time event processing engine. Stream Analytics makes it easy to set up real-time analytic computations on data streaming from devices, sensors, websites, social media, applications, infrastructure systems, and more.

The service can be hosted with a few clicks in the Azure portal; users can author a Stream Analytics job specifying the input source of the streaming data, the output sink for the results of your job, and a data transformation expressed in a SQL-like language. The jobs can be monitored and you can adjust the scale/speed of the job in the Azure portal to scale from a few kilobytes to a gigabyte or more of events processed per second.

Let's review how to configure Azure Stream Analytics step by step:

1. Log in to the Azure portal using your Azure credentials, click on **New**, and search for **Stream Analytics job**:

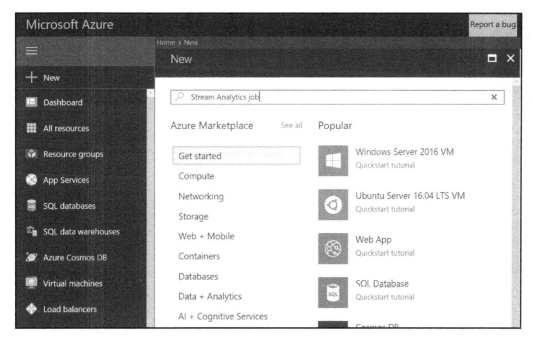

Creating new Stream Analytics job

2. Click on **Create** to create an Azure Stream Analytics instance:

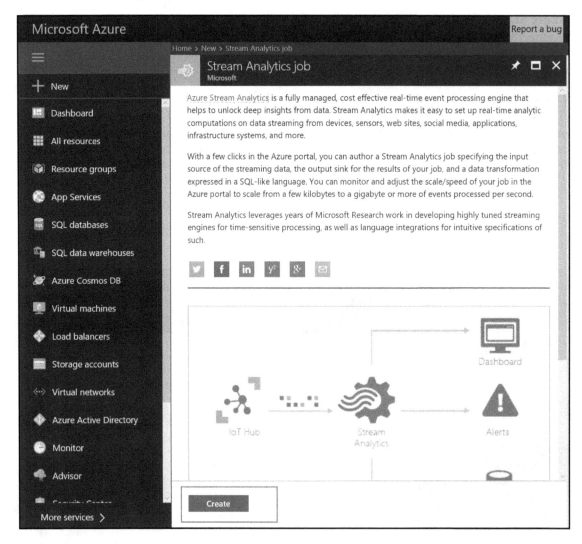

Creation of the Azure Stream Analytics deployment

3. Provide a **Job Name** and **Resource group name** for the Azure Stream Analytics job deployment:

Deploying the Azure Stream Analytics in new resource group

4. After a few minutes, the deployment will be complete:

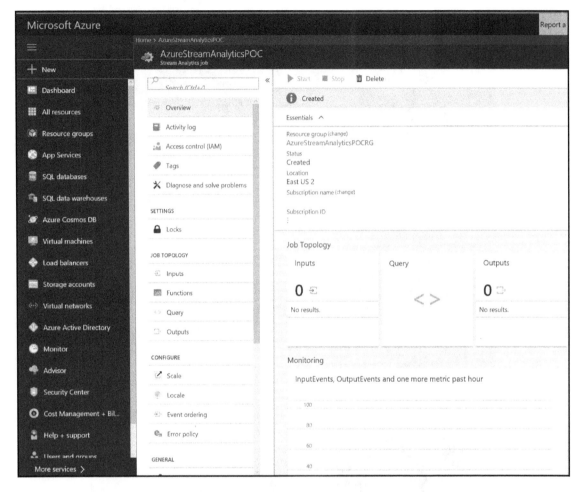

Service available for deployment

5. Review the following in the deployment—audit trail of the creation:

Audit Trail

6. Scale-out horizontally by adding more capacity using a simple UI:

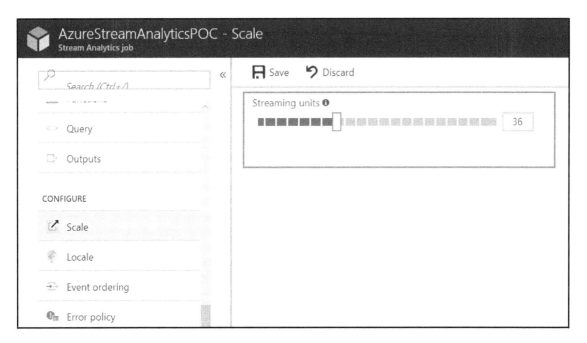

Scale up on demand using simple UI

7. Build in the Query interface to run queries:

Run SQL like Queries to ingest and process streaming data

8. Run Queries using a SQL-like interface, with the ability to accept late-arriving events with simple GUI-based configuration:

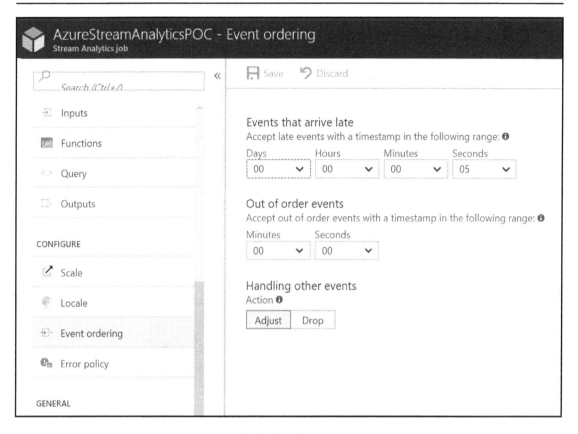

Configure late-arriving events

In this section, we created an Azure Stream Analytics instance and reviewed a couple of features. In the next sections, we will look into the advantages, security, and total cost of ownership.

Key advantages of Azure Stream Analytics

Let's quickly review how traditional streaming solutions are built; the core deployment starts with procuring and setting up the basic infrastructure necessary to host the streaming solution. Once this is done, we can then build the ingress and egress solution on top of the deployed infrastructure.

Once the core infrastructure is built, customer tools will be used to build **business intelligence** (**BI**) or machine-learning integration. After the system goes into production, scaling during runtime needs to be taken care of by capturing the telemetry and building and configuration of HW/SW resources as necessary. As business needs ramp up, so does the monitoring and troubleshooting.

The following screenshot illustrates how a traditional physical infrastructure based streaming solutions are built:

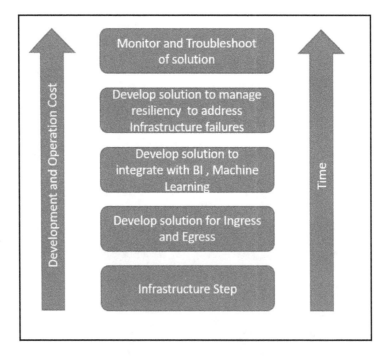

Traditional infrastructure model to deploy Streaming services

As we can see in the illustration following configuration, building and managing real-time Analytics solutions is super-easy and cost-effective with Azure Stream Analytics, which provides a fully managed, resilient, and scalable platform that allows customers to focus on business logic and not worry about infrastructure setup and management. SQL-like query language drastically reduces the learning curve and development cost for the developers:

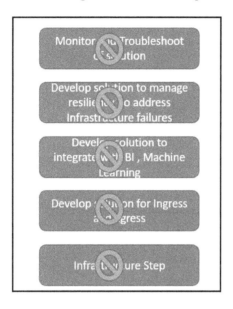

Azure Streaming Analytics is a PaaS solution and doesn't need any physical infrastructure components

Security

Azure Stream Analytics provides a number of inbuilt security mechanics in areas such as authentication, authorization, auditing, segmentation, and data protection. Let's quickly review them.

- Authentication support: Authentication support in Azure Stream Analytics is done at portal level. Users should have a valid subscription ID and password to access the Azure Stream Analytics job.

- Authorization: Authorization is the process during login where users provide their credentials (for example, user account name and password, smart card and PIN, Secure ID and PIN, and so on) to prove their Microsoft identity so that they can retrieve their access token from the authentication server. Authorization is supported by Azure Stream Analytics. Only authenticated/authorized users can access the Azure Stream Analytics job.
- Support for encryption: Data-at-rest using client-side encryption and TDE.
- Support for key management: Key management is supported through ingress and egress points.

Programmer productivity

One of the key features of Azure Stream Analytics is developer productivity, and it is driven a lot by the query language that is based on SQL constructs. It provides a wide array of functions for analytics on streaming data, all the way from simple data manipulation functions, data and time functions, temporal functions, mathematical, string, scaling, and much more. It provides two features natively out of the box. Let's review the features in detail in the next section:

- Declarative SQL constructs
- Built-in temporal semantics

Declarative SQL constructs

A simple-to-use UI is provided and queries can be constructed using the provided user interface. The following is the feature set of the declarative SQL constructs:

- Filters (Where)
- Projections (Select)
- Time-window and property-based aggregates (Group By)
- Time-shifted joins (specifying time bounds within which the joining events must occur)
- All combinations thereof

The following is a summary of different constructs to manipulate streaming data:

- **Data manipulation**: SELECT, FROM, WHERE GROUP BY, HAVING, CASE WHEN THEN ELSE, INNER/LEFT OUTER JOIN, UNION, CROSS/OUTER APPLY, CAST, INTO, ORDER BY ASC, DSC
- **Date and time functions**: DateName, DatePart, Day, Month, Year, DateDiff, DateTimeFromParts, DateAdd
- **Temporal functions**: Lag, IsFirst, LastCollectTop
- **Aggregate functions**: SUM, COUNT, AVG, MIN, MAX, STDEV, STDEVP, VAR VARP, TopOne
- **Mathematical functions**: ABS, CEILING, EXP, FLOOR POWER, SIGN, SQUARE, SQRT
- **String functions**: Len, Concat, CharIndex Substring, Lower Upper, PatIndex
- **Scaling extensions**: WITH, PARTITION BY OVER
- **Geospatial**: CreatePoint, CreatePolygon, CreateLineString, ST_DISTANCE, ST_WITHIN, ST_OVERLAPS, ST_INTERSECTS

Built-in temporal semantics

Azure Stream Analytics provides prebuilt temporal semantics to query time-based information and merge streams with multiple timelines. Here is a list of temporal semantics:

- Application or ingest timestamp
- Windowing functions
- Policies for event ordering
- Policies to manage latencies between ingress sources
- Manage streams with multiple timelines
- Join multiple streams of temporal windows
- Join streaming data with data-at-rest

Lowest total cost of ownership

Azure Stream Analytics is a fully managed PaaS service on Azure. There are no upfront costs or costs involved in setting up computer clusters and complex hardware wiring like you would do with an on-prem solution. It's a simple job service where there is no cluster provisioning and customers pay for what they use.

A key consideration is the variable workloads. With Azure Stream Analytics, you do not need to design your system for peak throughput and can add more compute footprint as you go.

If you have scenarios where data comes in spurts, you do not want to design a system for peak usage and leave it unutilized for other times. Let's say you are building a traffic monitoring solution—naturally, there is the expectation that it will expect peaks to show up during morning and evening rush hours. However, you would not want to design your system or investments to cater to these extremes. Cloud elasticity that Azure offers is a perfect fit here.

Azure Stream Analytics also offers fast recovery by checkpointing and at-least-once event delivery.

Here is a summary of the feature set:

- Zero upfront costs
- Up and running in seconds
- No SW or HW maintenance
- No performance tuning
- Pay only for usage
- Fully managed service
- No cluster topology management required
- Seamless scalability

Mission-critical and enterprise-less scalability and availability

Azure Stream Analytics is available across multiple worldwide data centers and sovereign clouds. Azure Stream Analytics promises 3-9s availability that is financially guaranteed with built-in auto recovery so that you will never lose the data. The good thing is customers do not need to write a single line of code to achieve this. The bottom-line is that enterprise readiness is built into the platform. Here is a summary of the Enterprise-ready features:

- Distributed scale-out architecture
- Ingests millions of events per second
- Accommodates variable loads
- Easily adds incremental resources to scale
- Available across multiple data centers and sovereign clouds

- Guaranteed events delivery
- Guaranteed 3-9s availability
- State management of auto recovery
- Scales using slider in Azure portal and not writing code
- Localization

Global compliance

In addition, Azure Stream Analytics is compliant with many industries and government certifications. It is already HIPPA-compliant built-in and suitable to host healthcare applications. That's how customers can scale up their businesses confidently. Here is a summary of global compliance:

- ISO 27001
- ISO 27018
- SOC 1 Type 2
- SOC 2 Type 2
- SOC 3 Type 2
- HIPAA/HITECH
- PCI DSS Level 1
- European Union Model Clauses
- China GB 18030

In the following sections, we will explore why Azure Stream Analytics is an integral part of the Cortana Intelligence suite and Azure IoT Hubs.

Microsoft Cortana Intelligence suite integration

Azure Stream Analytics is a part of the Cortana Intelligence suite. Why is there a need for a streaming solution within the Cortana intelligence suite? Take, for example, number of customers use Azure Stream Analytics to detect when their servers are down so that they can immediately go and patch or replace those servers to help their site performance and uptime. Data is coming from **System Center Operations Manager** (**SCOM**) events and other solutions to this real-time processing solution.

Stream Analytics detects anomalies and triggers system processes to create ServiceNow tickets or show them in live dashboards in real time to monitor the status of the system. In order to do this, you need everything in the Cortana Intelligence Suite (Dashboards, data movement, and so on) to work in concert with Azure Stream Analytics:

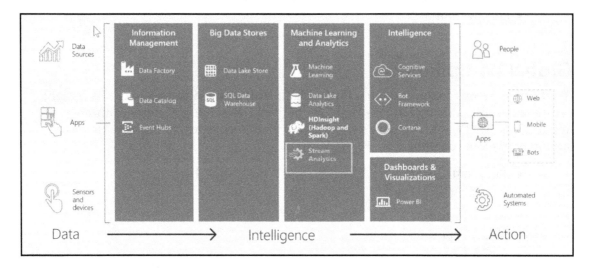

Cortana intelligence suite with Azure Stream Analytics

Azure IoT integration

Let's say you want to go and help a large car manufacturer with a connected cars scenario and give intelligent recommendations with predictive maintenance, and you integrate the IoT suite and Cortana Intelligence Suite. Stream Analytics helps bring both of these together to provide a unified solution:

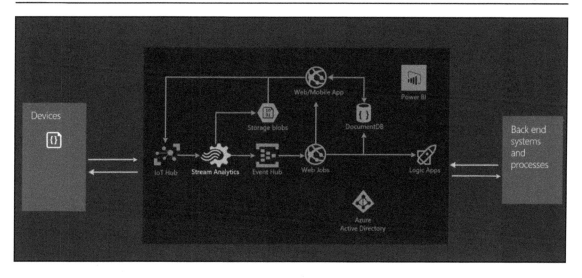

Azure IOT Integration with Azure Stream Analytics

As the preceding diagram illustrates, Azure Stream services support ingestion, analysis, and publishing of the result. In addition to these use cases, Azure Stream Analytics can be used for some of the more commonly known use cases like web analytics, fraud detection, recommendation engines, and preventive maintenance.

Summary

Following is a quick summary of topics we covered in this chapter. We reviewed what is Azure Stream Analytics, understood its key advantages in terms of developer productivity, ease of development and how to reduces total cost of ownership, global compliance certifications, the value of the PaaS based streaming solution to host mission-critical applications and briefly reviewed security.

Now that we have a basic understanding of Azure Stream Analytics in the next chapter we will explore how to start building a Streaming pipeline, look into deployment, logging and monitoring, and finally review sample use cases to consolidate our learnings.

3
Designing Real-Time Streaming Pipelines

In this chapter, we will look at the components that go into designing real-time streaming pipelines. We start with comparing stream and batch processing, followed by key streaming challenges, touch base on key streaming concepts. Traditional analytics solutions are designed around the concept of batch operations that move data between different persisted data stores. Users issue a query against the persisted data a rest to do ad hoc analysis, dashboards, or scorecards. This approach has been in use for a number of years and is still very much a relevant solution to business operations today.

To extract data insights on streaming data set requires a different type of approach and technology paradigm. We will focus on those aspects the next sections. First let's begin with a quick comparison between stream and batch processing.

Differencing stream processing and batch processing

The popularity of stream data platforms has been increasing significantly in recent times, due to the requirement of real-time access to information. Enterprises are transitioning parts of their data infrastructure from traditional batch processing to streaming paradigm due to changing business needs and the need to get of Real-Time Insights on data as business events occur.

It's critical to understand the fundamental differences between stream and batch processing:

	Stream Processing	Batch Processing
Data Volume	Smaller data chunks with a single or a small number of records.	Large volume, since data will be accumulated over a period of time and loaded incrementally in batches.
Query Processing	Queries are processed on a smaller subset of data. Usually based on the timestamp of the data arrival.	Queries are processed on an entire dataset.
Query Latency	Queries results are made available with extremely low latency—seconds or milliseconds.	Query results take a couple of minutes or hours, depending on the volume of data.
Data Insight	Stream processing ingests data close to real time and incrementally updates metrics and insights in response to each arriving data record.	The data is processed once a day or once every few hours and insights are not instantaneous.

The following list provides a subset of examples where a streaming data analytics solution can add value to a business:

- An online social media news publisher harvests streams of clickstream to aggregate and enriches the data with demographic data, to deliver relevancy and enhanced news experience to its audience.
- Real-time weather and traffic updates.
- Fraud prevention and detection on financial and non-financial transactions.
- Enhancing customer experience for an online retailer, food delivery, transportation and multitude of online businesses.
- Sensors in connected vehicles, farm machinery, heavy machinery and mechanical devices send data to a streaming application. The application monitors performance detects any potential defect in advance and places orders for required servicing (predictive maintenance), notifies field personal, service center to reach out to the customer. This enables manufacturers to become proactive rather than reactive.

Stream processing brings in a number of business advantages, like the following:

- Translate Real-Time Insights into a compelling customer experience.
- **Business Activity Monitoring** (**BAM**). Many large organizations have deep and complex processes. These processes need to be reconciled. These reconciliations are done using batch processing. With Stream Analytics, reconsolidations can happen in real time and this speeds up the business decision process.
- Provides more opportunity for traditional business to enhance and add value to their existing services. For example, if you are heavy equipment manufacture or servicing enterprise by introducing sensors and telemetry into the equipment, you can tap health of the machinery equipment in real time. This will enhance the value of the equipment and opens up net new opportunities to grow.

In the next sections, we will review components that go into designing real-time streaming solution and end the chapter with a canonical architecture. Let's start working on the concepts.

Logical flow of processing

In the current era of data explosion and requirement for an always-connected paradigm, organizations are collecting colossal volumes of data on a continuous basis in real or near-real-time basis. The value of this data surge depends on the ability to extract actionable and contextual insights in a timely fashion. Streaming applications have a very strong mandate to derive real-time actionable insights from massive data ingestion pipelines. They have to react to data in real time. For instance, as a data stream arrives, it should trigger a multitude of dependent actions and capture reactions. The most critical part of building streaming solutions is to understand the interlude between input, output and query processing at scale. Do also note streaming applications never exist in siloed mode, but part of the larger ecosystem of applications.

The following illustration provides a high-level conceptual view of various interplay with different components. Starting with a stream of data, reference data included to enrich the arriving streaming data, queries are executed and responses pushed out, followed by notifications to end users and storage of the final results in the data store for future references:

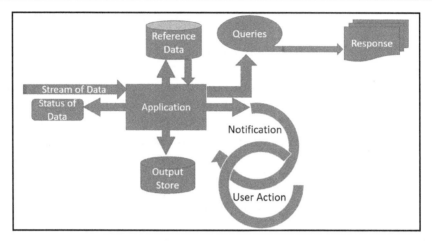

Logical view of streaming flow processing

If you take a traditional transactional data processing workload, all the data is collected before the start of processing. In the stream, processing queries are run against that data in flight as illustrated as follows:

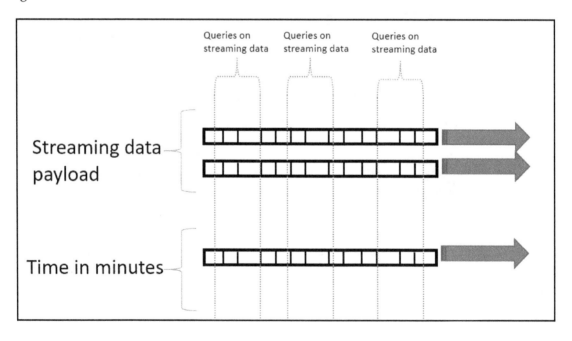

Queries executed on streaming data

When data is continually in motion keeping the state of the data is challenging or difficult, the state is stored in in-memory that is working memory and that is limited. Additionally, networking challenges will creep in turn resulting late arrival of data or missing data sets. Patterns like Command Query Responsibility Segregation is used to scale out read and writes separately.

Command Query Responsibility Segregation (**CQRS**) is an architecture pattern for separating concerns, the reads and writes are separated and provides the ability to read and write faster in separate streams. The event stored in the event store is immutable with a timestamp.

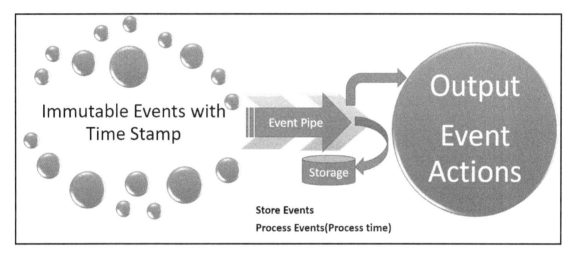

In the preceding architecture, immutable events with data stamp are sent through the event pipe and split between immediate event action and long-term data retention. Events are stored with a timestamp and it gives the ability to determine the state of the system at any previous point in time by querying the Events. By splitting the data streams into multiple channels higher throughput is achieved.

Out of order and late arrival of data

There are a number of scenarios, due to connectivity and networking reasons events generated by source application will arrive out of order or arrive late. For example in IoT scenario, the connected devices can suffer from intermediate connectivity in which case a set of data will be held on the device that is waiting for a connection to be re-established before the burst is transmitted, forecasting intermittent device connectivity reliably is a lot more difficult. The streaming solution should have the capacity to handle out of order events. The out of order flow is showcased as following for easier understanding:

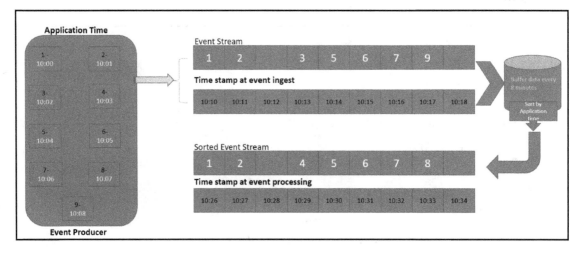

Out of order event

In the **Internet of Things (IoT)** scenarios, there will be device level challenges that affecting the application at the event source due to a number of reasons. The event data will reach bit later than anticipated time. Following illustration showcases the late arrival events:

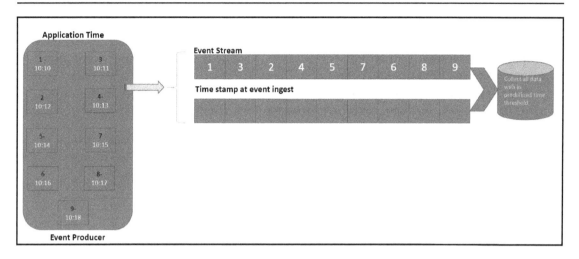

Late arriving events

The event processing system should have pre-configured logic to handle out of order and late arrival events.

Session grouping and windowing challenges

To illustrate the concept, let's take an example of a stockbroking firm that actively monitors stock markets, stock trader activity, and customer accounts. Each trader will have an application that keeps tracks of moving average of an investment portfolio of his/her clients. The net worth of the customer portfolio will constantly change as the market trading happens.

In the same context, if we look into backend systems at the stock exchange floor it will extract information from the multitude of feeds and correlate these events to infer market variables and sentiment, in turn, impacting the stock prices.

If a trader initiates a buy, sell, or lock in stock based on the information he sees on his screen. The locked in price for buy or sell shouldn't be changed.

At the end of the trading day, all the events (buy, sell, consolidation) should be processed in exact order to ensure that they are accurate and don't breach any security trading rules and reconcile all the data in the same order is received and processed.

In real-time applications as our example, a common requirement is to perform set-based computation like aggregation or other operations over subsets of events that fall within a given period in the same sequence the events were received. In the real-time event, the concept of time is a fundamental necessity to the event-based processing systems. It's important to have a simple way to work with the time component of query logic in the system. This is where session grouping and windowing concepts come into play.

Windowing is to represent groupings by time. A window contains event data along a timeline and enables you to perform various operations against the events within that window and every window operation outputs event at the end of the window.

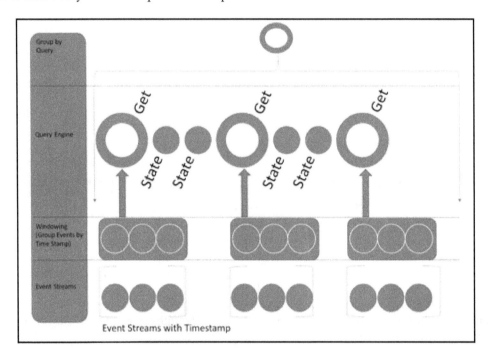

Event Streams with Timestamp

Windowing enables computational operations on moving datasets. One technique is to use some of the metadata from the streams, like timestamp, and build a grouping of data. For instance traditional databases (RDBMS), the state is stored and the query engine utilizes them to return the dataset. Due to the dynamic model of the streaming, the stream query processing engine should have the ability to build and maintain states for flowing events. There are 3 types of windows: Tumbling, Hopping and Sliding, we will cover in the next few chapter. All streaming solution should be able to cater extensive windowing requirements. Next, we move on to reviewing message consistency concepts.

Message consistency

In loosely coupled and asynchronous systems, message queuing is widely used. Distributed systems are loosely coupled systems. This leads to the challenge of messages, events, or records in one part of the system getting processed or pushed earlier than some other parts of the system, thus leading to nonsensical results. Streaming systems are built to deliver messages with throughput across a wide spectrum of latencies and strong consistency guarantees. For example, stream processing systems are characterized by at least once, at most once, and exactly once processing semantics. These are important characteristics that should be carefully considered from the point of view of consistency and durability in a stream processing application. Let's briefly look into message delivery semantics:

At most once delivery [0,1]	No commitment to deliver the messages or redelivery
At least once delivery [1 .. n]	Messages will never be lost, but messages may be redelivered
Exactly once delivery [1]	Messages will never be lost, messages are never redelivered

Fault tolerance, recovery, and storage

Building redundant, fault-tolerant, and highly performant stream processing is hard. In traditional batch processing, when a job fails, we just retry or re-run either the failed components or a small portion of the failed job. The batch job world operates on the assumption that data is fixed and finite. The underlying infrastructure is built on that immutable data model. The worst case scenario is that the batch job has to be run from the beginning to the end again.

Similar to traditional business analytics solutions, the architecture for real-time event processing is based on the pattern of data ingestion, processing, and ultimately notification/presentation by either the end users or other applications. The streaming solution should have an inbuilt capability to store the data in redundant working memory, recover from processing failure and ability to compensate for infrastructure, networks etc.

The following image provides a high-level explanation of the end-to-end architecture and a summary of the roles that each of these layers fulfills:

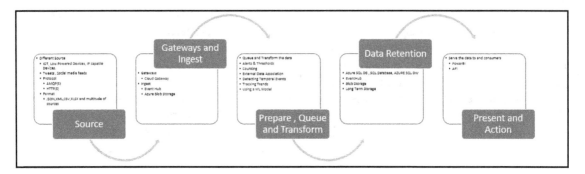

Source

The source represents the multitude of systems that can generate events and data for processing. The scale and volume of where and how much data can be generated is incredibly vast. For instance, a given event can come from a single IP device, smartphone, machines, or computer appliance. One important point to consider is how these systems deliver these events.

The delivery could be the batch mode, streamed out or pushed asynchronously as and when connectivity is made available. Given the vastness of the source, the data format also varies, as does the communication protocol (Http(s), **Advanced Message Queuing Protocol (AMQP)**).The origin of data can be varied, from public sources to social media feeds to the internal data source. The streaming solution should be able to handle different type of protocols, we will review that in the next section.

Communication and collection

Communication plays a key role in connecting the source and destination. Gateway plays an important/essential role in connecting an external device to the processing engine. Standard protocols, like HTTP(s), AMQP, and MQTT, enable connectivity between the device and the processing engine.

HTTP(S) and AMQP were developed in the financial industry to overcome some of the inefficiencies found in HTTP. AMQP is more efficient in terms of latency and throughput. Do note that HTTP(S) can be used as the transport layer.

Ingest, queue, and transform

Data ingestion is about storing the streaming data into a storage system for analysis. The ingestion can be either synchronous or asynchronous, depending on the source and the destination. Having a robust, efficient, and performant ingestion system will help keep the focus on analysis, instead of data preparation and transformation. After being acquired and ingested, the data can travel into two types of path: hot path and cold path, we will review them briefly in the next section.

Hot path

The hot data is subjected to real-time analysis based on a set of rules, and the data is transformed and insights are generated. The data is usually looked from the viewpoint of event time to generate accurate predictions. As an additional step, the data can be applied to machine learning models to better produce the desired output or prediction. The key value of the hot path data is the notification that gets generated based on the data. Review the high level:

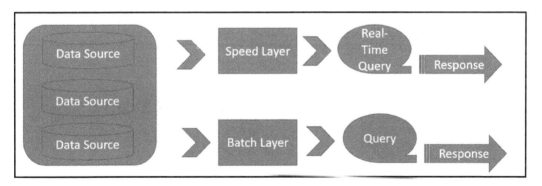

Cold path

The cold path is where the data is moved into storage and then different analytic services will be used to generate insights. A key attribute of the cold path data is data is read-only and is used for reporting purposes:

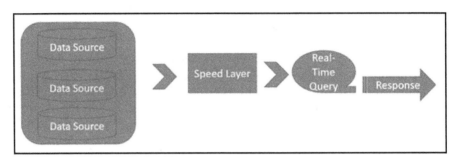

Data retention

The streaming model represents a significant shift in data processing, moving from a point in time queries against stationary data to querying moving data. Data is persisted is primarily to store the result set from the queries for future reference. The streaming system should have the ability to write to a variety of destinations, such as object storage, RDBMS, NoSQL, or even back to the streaming engine as input for other services.

Do note, there will be a number of downstream applications that depend on this data:

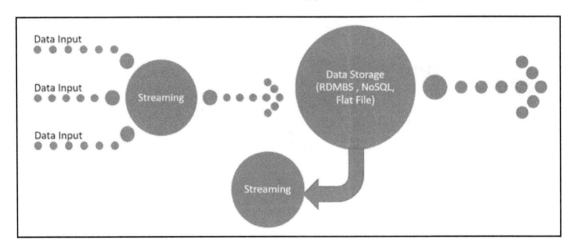

Presentation and action

With a streaming dataset, there is no underlying database or storage and everything will be processed in memory due to low latency requirement. Streaming systems should provide the ability to store the data on persistent storage to run reports at the later stage. For instance, Azure provides an ability to store the data in SQL Storage and reporting using Power BI.

We will go deeper into reporting based on streaming data in the coming chapters.

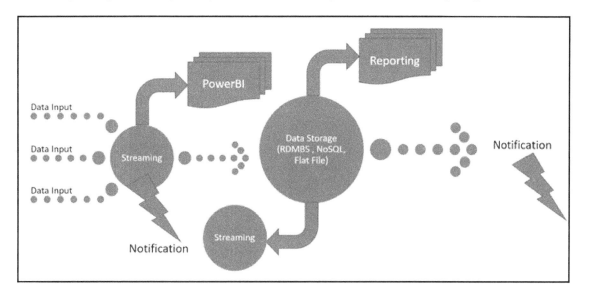

Canonical Azure architecture

The following architecture is a well know canonical design pattern for streaming data, let's review the components of the architecture:

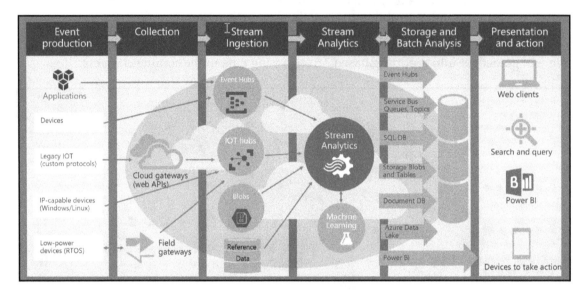

- **Input**: Inputs are the sources of events. Note that the **original** sources of streaming events are devices, machines, applications, sensors, applications, and so on. However, ASA is not intended to connect to them directly. Rather, ASA lets Azure Event Hubs be the primary interface to the wide variety of event sources. ASA is optimized to get streaming data from Azure Event Hubs and Azure Blob storage. Azure Blob storage is the likely place where log or reference data is stored. The list of input sources that ASA directly integrates with may increase in the future, but Azure Event Hubs and Azure Blob storage will be the primary sources. There can be multiple inputs used in each Stream Analytics job that can come from Azure Event Hubs and Azure Blob storage.

- **Query**: Queries are the main component of an ASA application. They implement the **analytics logic**. They are a set of transformations that are applied to the input stream to produce another set of output events. Queries are the only thing that ASA application developers actually develop. Everything else is done through guided wizards in the Azure Portal. Note that ASA has a SQL-like query language, but unlike traditional databases, ASA queries run continuously against the stream of incoming events. The queries stop being applied only when the job itself stops.

- **Output**: As queries execute, they continuously produce results. The results can be stored in Blob storage, Event Hubs, Azure Tables, and Azure SQL database. Note that if the output is stored in Event Hub or Blob storage, it can become the input to another ASA job. So it is possible to chain together multiple jobs to implement a series of transformations. A single ASA job can output to multiple permanent stores.

Summary

In this chapter, we learned about the key components of designing real-time streaming pipelines, Stream Analytics and type of streaming components required to build robust streaming solutions and some of the challenges. In the next chapters, we will start to take a detailed look at designing and building real-time event processing using Azure Stream Analytics.

4
Developing Real-Time Event Processing with Azure Streaming

In this chapter, we will explore end-to-end development concepts with guidance related to Azure Stream Analytics job implementation, introducing various development tools to build streaming jobs on the cloud, provisioning through the Azure portal, and utilization techniques of **Azure Resource Management** (**ARM**) templates to work with Stream Analytics jobs in a real-world scenario.

The following points of discussion in this chapter are as follows:

- Step-by-step implementation guidance for a real-world streaming job on Azure using Streaming Analytics tools for Visual Studio
- The provisioning details of a Stream Analytics job using the Azure portal
- Development illustrations related to a streaming job using the Azure Resource Manager template
- Introduction to various input data sources and output sink connectors for Azure Stream Analytics

Stream Analytics tools for Visual Studio

The Stream Analytics tools for Visual Studio help prepare, build, and deploy real-time events on Azure. Optionally, the tools enable you to monitor the streaming job using local sample data as job input testing as well as real-time monitoring, job metrics, diagram view, and so on. This tool provides a complete development setup for the implementation and deployment of real-world Azure Stream Analytics jobs using Visual Studio.

Prerequisites for the installation of Stream Analytics tools

This following development environment setup is needed in order to start working with Azure Stream Analytics jobs using Visual Studio:

- Visual Studio supported versions: Visual Studio 2017/2015 (Enterprise, Professional, or Ultimate, and Community Edition), Visual Studio 2013 updated with Edition 4 (all Editions except Express), or VS 2012 Enterprise
- Azure SDK for .NET version 2.7.1 or later is compulsory, which can be downloaded from `https://azure.microsoft.com/en-us/downloads/`.
- The Stream Analytics tool for VS can be downloaded from `https://www.microsoft.com/en-us/download/details.aspx?id=54630`.

Development of a Stream Analytics job using Visual Studio

Post the installation of the Stream Analytics tool, a new stream analytics job can be created in Visual Studio.

1. You can get started in Visual Studio IDE from **File | New Project**. Under the **Templates**, select **Stream Analytics** and choose **Azure Stream Analytics Application**.
2. Next, the job name, project, and solution location should be provided. Under **Solution** menu, you may also select options such as **Add to solution** or **Create new instance** apart from **Create new solution** from the available drop-down menu during Visual Studio Stream Analytics job creation:

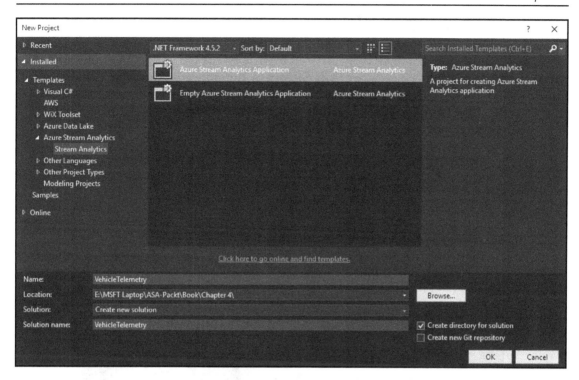

3. Once the ASA job is created, in the **Solution Explorer**, the job topology folder structure could be viewed as **Inputs** (job input), **Outputs** (job output), `JobConfig.json`, `Script.asaql` (Stream Analytics Query file), Azure Functions (optional), and so on:

4. Next, provide the job topology data input and output event source settings by selecting **Input.json** and **Output.json** from **Inputs** and **Outputs** directories, respectively. For example, you need to provide the job input alias name and select source type as either **Data Stream** or **Reference Stream**. The data stream defines the unlimited events of complex streams that process over Azure Service Bus Event Hub, IoT Hub, or Blob storage. The Reference Stream data is static in nature, limited to only 100 MB in size.

> As of writing this book, only the Azure Blob storage type job input is supported by Reference Data.

5. For a **Vehicle Telemetry Predictive Analysis** demo using an Azure Stream Analytics job, we need to take two different job data streams. One should be a Stream type for an illimitable sequence of real-time events processed through Azure Event Hub along with Hub policy name, policy key, event serialization format, and so on:

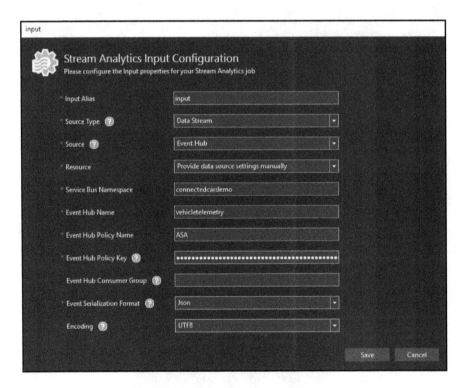

6. For a reference stream also, a new job input stream JSON file could be added by right-clicking the **Inputs** folder and then **Add** then select **New Item**. Provide the configuration file name to define static vehicle reference data from an auxiliary data file like CSV stored in Azure Blob storage:

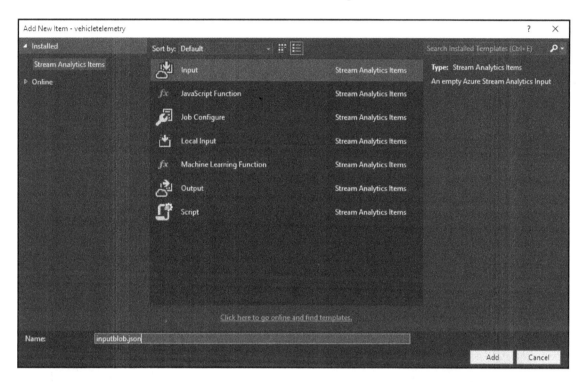

7. You need to provide the job input configuration properties for the Reference Data Stream from Azure Blob storage as well by modifying data stream as Reference data along with the Blob storage account name, key, path pattern, and container name:

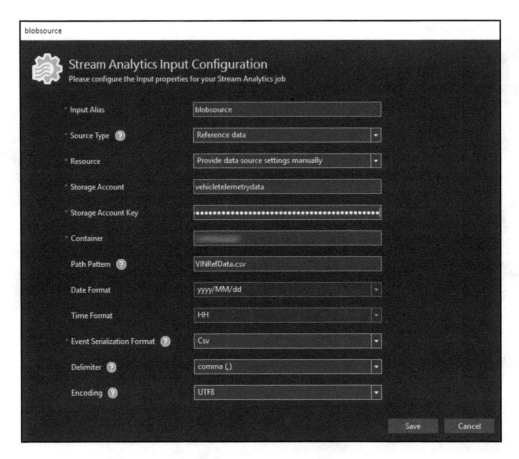

8. Now, you can assert the job topology output settings by selecting the Output.json file under the **Outputs** folder of the Stream Analytics job project under VS Solution Explorer. Provide the job output type as Blob storage and share the storage account name, key, container name, and path pattern. Optionally, you may select other job output types as well as SQL database, Event Hub, Azure Table storage, Service Bus Queue or Topic, Cosmos DB, and so on. You must need to **Save** the wizards once the job input and output configuration properties are set.

As of writing this book, Power BI and Azure Data Lake Store are not supported yet as Stream analytics job topology output using ASA tools for Visual Studio.

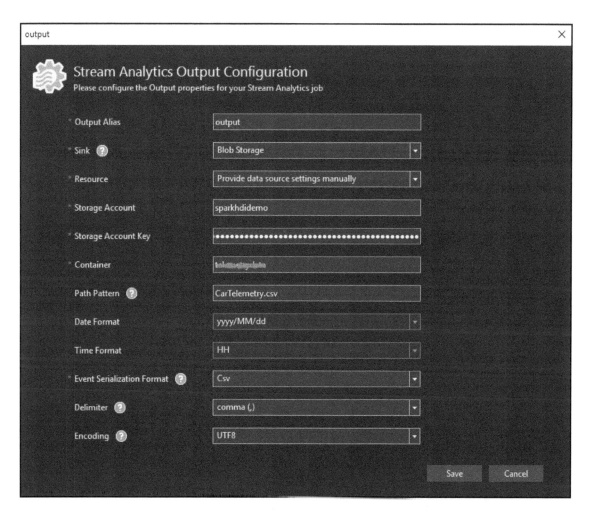

Defining a Stream Analytics query for Vehicle Telemetry job analysis using Stream Analytics tools

To assign the streaming analytics query definition, the `Script.asasql` file from the ASA project should be selected by specifying the data and reference stream input joining operation along with supplying analyzed output to Blob storage as configured in job properties.

Query to define Vehicle Telemetry (Connected Car) engine health status and pollution index over cities

For connected car and real-time predictive Vehicle Telemetry Analysis, there's a necessity to specify opportunities for new solutions in terms of how a car could be shipped globally with the required smart hardware to connect to the internet within the next few years. How the embedded connections could define Vehicle Telemetry predictive health status so automotive companies will be able to collect data on the performance of cars, to send interactive updates and patches to car's instrumentation remotely, and just to avoid car equipment damage with precautionary measures with prior notification through intelligent vehicle health telemetry analysis using Azure Streaming.

The solution architecture of the Connected Car—Vehicle Telemetry Analysis case study used in this demo, with Azure Stream Analytics for real-time predictive analysis, is as follows:

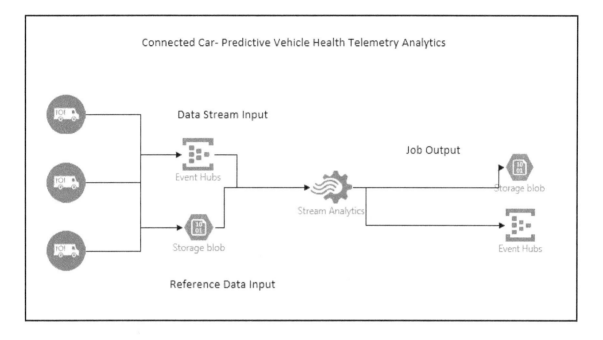

Testing Stream Analytics queries locally or in the cloud

Azure Stream Analytics tools in Visual Studio offer the flexibility to execute the queries either locally or directly in the cloud. In the `Script.asaql` file, you need to provide the respective query of your streaming job and test against local input stream/Reference data for query testing before processing in Azure:

1. To run the Stream Analytics job query locally, first select **Add Local Input** by right-clicking on the ASA project in VS **Solution Explorer**, and choose to **Add Local Input**:

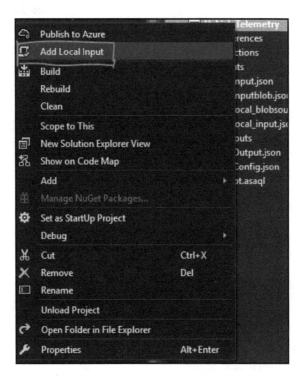

2. Define the local input for each Event Hub Data Stream and Blob storage data and execute the job query locally before publishing it in Azure:

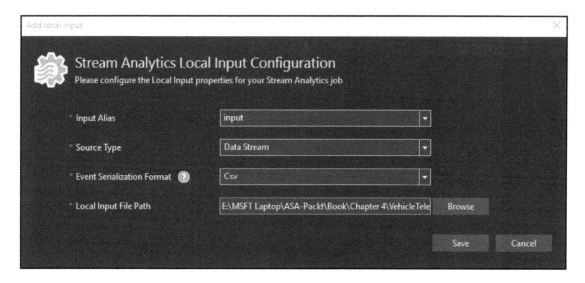

3. After adding each local input test data, you can test the Stream Analytics job query locally in VS editor by clicking on the **Run Locally** button in the top left corner of VS IDE:

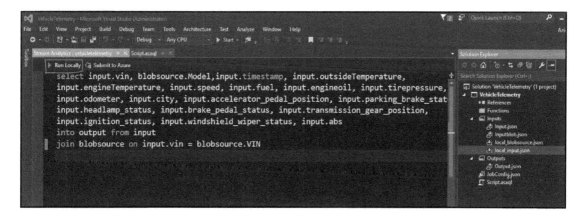

4. For Connected Car-Predictive Vehicle Telemetry Analysis to determine basic vehicle health hardware analysis, it's important to analyze the following telemetry indexes:

    *   Vehicle diagnostic
    *   Usage-based insurance
    *   Engine emission control
    *   Engine performance remapping
    *   Eco-driving
    *   Roadside assistance call
    *   Fleet management

    So, specify the following schema during the designing of a connected car streaming job query with Stream Analytics using parameters such as Vehicle Index no, Model, outside temperature, engine speed, fuel meter, tire pressure, and brake status, by defining INNER join with Event Hub data streams along with Blob storage reference streams containing vehicle model information:

```
Select input.vin, BlobSource.Model, input.timestamp,
input.outsideTemperature,
input.engineTemperature, input.speed, input.fuel,
input.engineoil,
input.tirepressure, input.odometer, input.city,
input.accelerator_pedal_position,
input.parking_brake_status,
input.headlamp_status, input.brake_pedal_status,
input.transmission_gear_position, input.ignition_status,
input.windshield_wiper_status, input.abs into output from
input join BlobSource
on input.vin = BlobSource.VIN
```

    The query could be further customized for complex event processing analysis in terms of defining windowing concepts like Tumbling window function, which assigns equal length non-overlapping series of events in streams with a fixed time slice.

The following Vehicle Telemetry analytics query will specify a smart car health index parameter with complex streams from a specified two-second timestamp interval in the form of a fixed length series of events:

```
select BlobSource.Model, input.city,count(vin) as cars,
avg(input.engineTemperature) as engineTemperature,
avg(input.speed) as Speed, avg(input.fuel) as Fuel,
avg(input.engineoil) as EngineOil,avg(input.tirepressure)
as TirePressure, avg(input.odometer) as Odometer
 into EventHubOut from input join BlobSource
on input.vin = BlobSource.VIN group by BlobSource.model,
input.city, TumblingWindow(second,2)
```

5. The query could be executed locally or submitted to Azure. While running the job locally, a Command Prompt will appear asserting the local Stream Analytics job's running status, with the output data folder location:

```
C:\WINDOWS\system32\CMD.exe                                                    —  □  ×
============================= Start local run ===================================
09/23/2017 10:22:26 PM : Info : There is 2 input(s) for job
09/23/2017 10:22:26 PM : Info : Input Alias : 'blobsource' , Input Type : 'Reference data'
09/23/2017 10:22:26 PM : Info : Input Alias : 'input' , Input Type : 'Data Stream'
09/23/2017 10:22:26 PM : Info : Begin to compile script ....
09/23/2017 10:22:27 PM : Info : Compile job script successfully.
09/23/2017 10:22:27 PM : Info : Begin to construct query inputs ...
09/23/2017 10:22:27 PM : Info : Detecting several necessary inputs for running this script : input,blobsource
09/23/2017 10:22:27 PM : Info : Construct query inputs successfuly
09/23/2017 10:22:27 PM : Info : Begin to execute query ...
09/23/2017 10:22:28 PM : Info : Execute query successfully
09/23/2017 10:22:28 PM : Info : There is 1 output(s) for job
09/23/2017 10:22:28 PM : Info : Create file E:\MSFT Laptop\ASA-Packt\Book\Chapter 4\VehicleTelemetry\VehicleTelemetry\AS
ALocalRun\2017-09-23-22-22-26\output.csv for : output
09/23/2017 10:22:28 PM : Info : Create file E:\MSFT Laptop\ASA-Packt\Book\Chapter 4\VehicleTelemetry\VehicleTelemetry\AS
ALocalRun\2017-09-23-22-22-26\output.json for : output
=============== Local run successfully : save all output result to E:\MSFT Laptop\ASA-Packt\Book\Chapter 4\VehicleTeleme
try\VehicleTelemetry\ASALocalRun\2017-09-23-22-22-26 ===================
Press any key to continue . . .
```

6. If run locally, the job output folder would contain two files in the project disk location within the `ASALocalRun` directory named, with the current date timestamp. Two output files would be present in `.csv` and `.json` formats respectively:

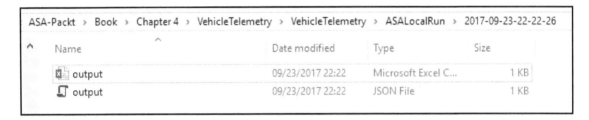

Now, if submitted the job to Azure from the Stream Analytics project in Visual Studio, it offers a beautiful job dashboard while providing an interactive job diagram view, job metrics graph, and errors (if any).

The Vehicle Telemetry Predictive Health Analytics job dashboard in Visual Studio provides a nice job diagram with Real-Time Insights of events, with a display refreshed at a minimum rate of every 30 minutes:

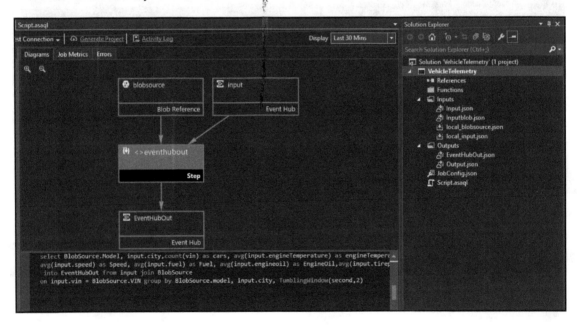

The Stream Analytics job metrics graph provides interactive insights on input and output events, out of order events, late events, runtime errors, and data conversion errors related to the job as appropriate:

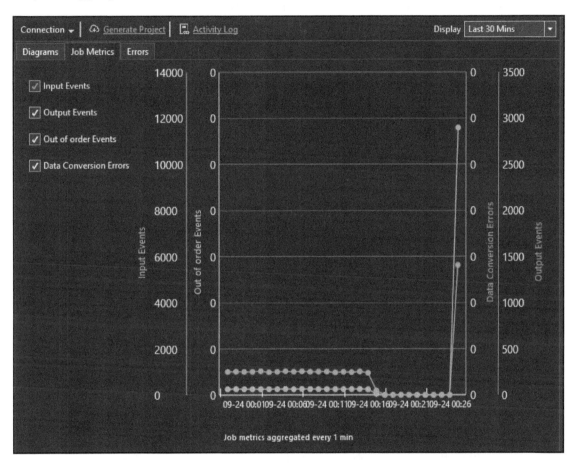

For Connected Car-Predictive Vehicle Telemetry Analytics, you may configure the data input streams processed with complex events by using a definite timestamp interval in a non-overlapping mode such as Tumbling window over a two-second time slicer. The output sink should be configured as Service Bus Event Hub in a data partitioning unit of 32, with a maximum message retention period of 7 days. The output job sink processed events in Event Hub could be archived as well in Azure blob storage for a long-term infrequent access perspective:

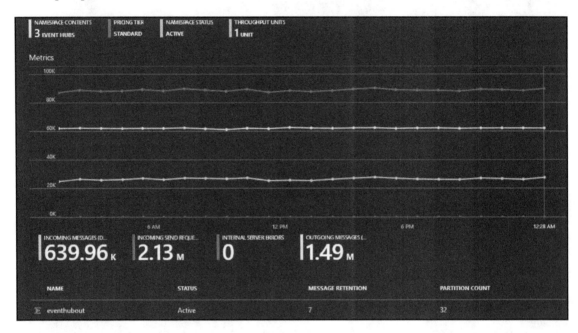

The Azure Service Bus, Event Hub job output metrics dashboard view configured for vehicle telemetry analysis is as follows:

- On the left side of the job dashboard, the **Job Summary** provides a comprehensive view controller of the job parameters such as job status, creation time, job output start time, start mode, last output timestamp, output error handling mechanism provided for quick reference logs, late event arrival tolerance windows, and so on. The job can be stopped and started, deleted, or even refreshed by selecting icons from the top left menu of the job view dashboard in VS:

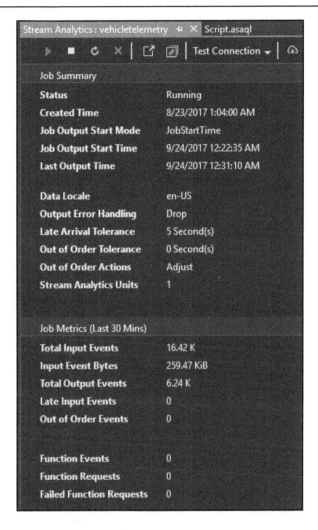

Optionally, a Stream Analytics complete project clone can also be generated by clicking on the **Generate Project** icon from the top menu of the job dashboard.

Stream Analytics job configuration parameter settings in Visual Studio

Stream Analytics tools for Visual Studio also allows job performance monitoring and management with optimization configuration mechanisms to be handled within the development environment itself. Inside the solution explorer of the ASA project, the file `JobConfig.json` or `Configuration.json` (in the generated ASA project) provides optimization and management monitoring settings like Streaming Units allocation, configuration of **Out of Order Actions** as **Adjust** or **Drop**, **Data Locale**, **Output Error Handling** as **Drop** or **Retry** mechanism, and **Out of Order Tolerance Window** or **Late Arrival Tolerance Window** intervals settings:

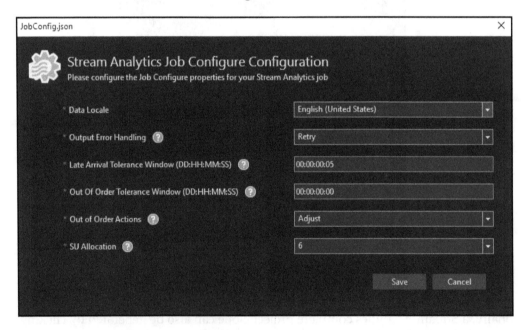

A streaming unit in an Azure Stream Analytics job can be optimized by default up to the value of 48 **Streaming Unit** (**SU**). Streaming Unit defines the resources and computation capability to execute a streaming analytics job complex event processing with blended measures of hardware compute powers like CPU, memory, and read/write throughput rate specifying a basic unit of job scaling ability. By default, each Azure subscription comes with a quota limit of 50 SU for all of the analytics jobs in a specified region basis. If you require SU consumption beyond 48 SU, please contact Microsoft support.

Implementation of an Azure Stream Analytics job using the Azure portal

Azure Stream Analytics is a fully managed complex event processing real-time data analytics computation engine that works on a continuous stream of data. On the job architecture level, it consists of event source (Input), sink (Output), and real-time job queries for transformation. The Stream Analytics job in Azure can also be created using the Azure portal (`https://portal.azure.com/`):

1. To get started with provisioning an Azure Stream Analytics job from the portal, select **New** and, under **Azure Marketplace**, choose either the **Data + Analytics** or **Internet of Things** option, and then click on **Stream Analytics job**:

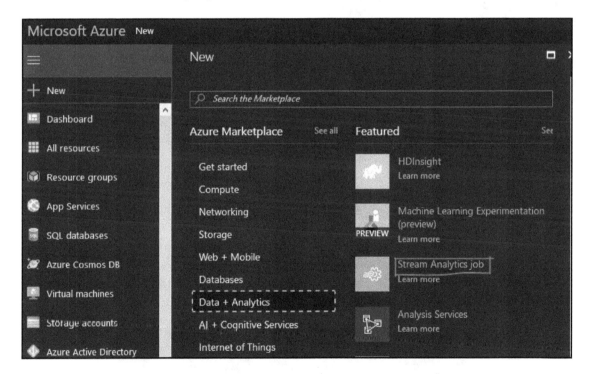

2. Define the job name and choose the appropriate Azure subscription. Then create a new Azure **Resource group** or choose an existing resource groupset. Azure Resource group is a logical unit container that consists of multiple Azure-managed services together under the same resource manager.

3. Finally, provide the **Location**, in case the Stream Analytics job is getting provisioned in a new resource group, and click on the **Create** button to start the implementation of a Stream Analytics job:

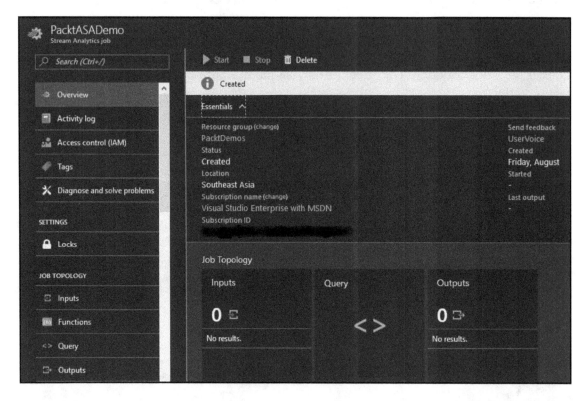

4. Optionally, the **Pin to dashboard** menu can be checked so that a shortcut file is created on the portal dashboard.

5. The progress of stream analytics job provisioning can be tracked on the Azure portal under notification hub:

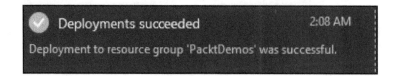

6. By default, the Stream Analytics job is created without any job input, output, and query configuration settings. The job will have the **Created** status and the **Start**, **Stop** option is disabled. Once the job input data source, output sink, and query are configured, then the job can be started.

 As of writing this book, provisioning of the Azure Stream Analytics job using the Azure classic portal (`https://manage.windowsazure.com`) has been deprecated and Stream Analytics job can be created using Azure Resource Manager model only.

Provisioning for an Azure Stream Analytics job using the Azure Resource Manager template

Azure Stream Analytics jobs can be provisioned using the ARM template, which is a bunch of REST API services invoked to create, test, and deploy various Azure resources implemented under the same resource group logical container. In fact, while provisioning Stream Analytics job using Azure Portal UI, it invokes ARM-based REST API services to create the streaming job with default configuration parameter settings.

Azure ARM Template - Infrastructure as code

Azure Resource Manager (ARM 2.0) template offers to manage a process life cycle of maintaining and implementing infrastructure resources in a JSON-based declarative manner, including appropriate definition and parameter configuration files instead of the traditional legacy approach and providing a better **Continuous Integration (CI)/Continuous Deployment (CD)** process.

Azure ARM as Infrastructure as code provides the facility of JSON resource templates reusability for repeatable or similar environment deployment, maintaining a consistency in script definition blocks with a rapid acceleration deployment approach. Further, it specifies flexibility by integrating additional configuration in JSON resource deployment code definitions in terms of extensibility.

Getting started with provisioning Azure Stream Analytics job using the ARM template

Visual Studio provides an option to provision Stream Analytics job using the Azure Resource Group deployment template with the help of Azure SDK. The template is a logical container of JSON resource code definitions and parameter settings with artifacts necessary for an ARM to create the ASA job environment and deploy to Azure:

1. From the Visual Studio **New Project** option under installed templates, select **Cloud** and choose **Azure Resource Group** to start creating the ARM template for the deployment of the Stream Analytics job. Provide the name of the project and its location on the local disk:

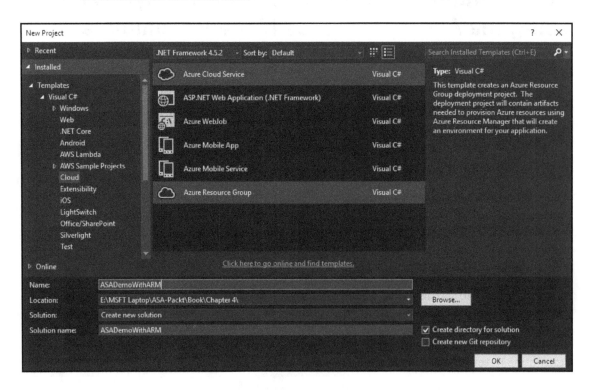

2. After creating the project, a prompt will appear to select Azure resource templates from the quick-start templates gallery. Select **Azure QuickStart (github.com/Azure/azure-quickstart-templates)** and search for `Stream Analytics`. The Stream Analytics template will come out; click on **OK** to complete the creation of the Stream Analytics project definition in VS:

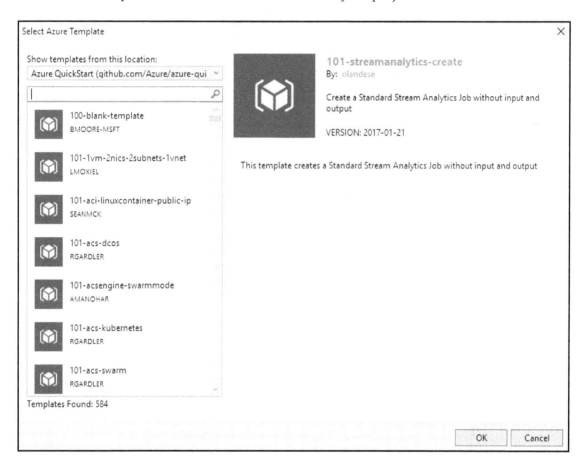

3. After ARM project created in Visual Studio for Stream Analytics, the project in Solution Explorer consists of a few JSON deployment scripts (`azuredeploy.json`, `azuredeploy.parameters.json`) along with an ARM-PowerShell script for deployment of the resource:

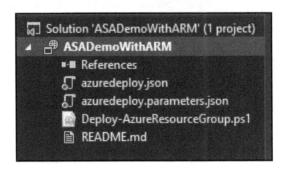

4. `azuredeploy.json`: This file consists of ARM schema, content version, and resource parameter settings along with detailed Stream Analytics job configurations such as `numberOfStreamingUnits`, input and output job topology resources along with job name, location, SKU specification, computation parameters, query transformation properties, and query definitions. The expressions and functions contained within these `azureploy.json` and `azuredeploy-parameters.json` files are evaluated and executed during resource deployment:

```
{
  "$schema":
"http://schema.management.azure.com/schemas/2015-01-01/deploymentTe
mplate.json",
  "contentVersion": "1.1.0.0",
  "parameters": {
  "streamAnalyticsJobName": {
  "type": "string",
  "minLength": 3,
  "maxLength": 63,
  "metadata": {
  "description": "Stream Analytics Job Name, can contain
alphanumeric characters and hypen and must be 3-63 characters long"
  }
  },
  "numberOfStreamingUnits": {
  "type": "int",
  "minValue": 1,
  "maxValue": 48,
  "allowedValues": [
```

```
      1,
      3,
      6,
      12,
      18,
      24,
      30,
      36,
      42,
      48
      ],
      "metadata": {
      "description": "Number of Streaming Units"
      }
      }
      },
      "resources": [
      {
      "type": "Microsoft.StreamAnalytics/StreamingJobs",
      "apiVersion": "2016-03-01",
      "name": "[parameters('streamAnalyticsJobName')]",
      "location": "[resourceGroup().location]",
      "properties": {
      "sku": {
      "name": "standard"
      },
      "outputErrorPolicy": "stop",
      "eventsOutOfOrderPolicy": "adjust",
      "eventsOutOfOrderMaxDelayInSeconds": 0,
      "eventsLateArrivalMaxDelayInSeconds": 5,
      "dataLocale": "en-US",
      "inputs": [],
      "transformation": {
      "name": "Transformation",
      "properties": {
      "streamingUnits": "[parameters('numberOfStreamingUnits')]",
      "query": "SELECT\r\n *\r\nINTO\r\n [YourOutputAlias]\r\nFROM\r\n
[YourInputAlias]"
      }
      }
      }
      }
      ]
      }
```

5. `azuredeploy-parameters.json`: The job names, with the number of scaling unit (Streaming Unit) configuration settings, are designed in this file:

```
{
  "$schema":
"http://schema.management.azure.com/schemas/2015-01-01/deploymentPa
rameters.json#",
  "contentVersion": "1.1.0.0",
  "parameters": {
  "streamAnalyticsJobName": {
  "value": "packtasajob"
  },
  "numberOfStreamingUnits": {
  "value": 1
  }
  }
}
```

Deployment and validation of the Stream Analytics ARM template to Azure Resource Group

In order to validate and deploy the Stream Analytics ARM project to the Azure environment, right-click on the project and select **Validate** (just to validate the ARM template configuration settings) or choose to deploy to publish the stream analytics job to Azure:

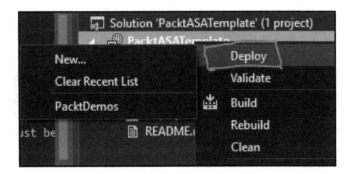

- For the deployment of the project template with artifacts, from **Deploy**, select
  New and provide an Azure Resource Group name, or select an existing Resource
  Group to deploy the Stream Analytics ARM template to Azure for provisioning.
  It will first validate the ARM template and then start creating the Azure
  environment deployment, which can be monitored from the VS output window:

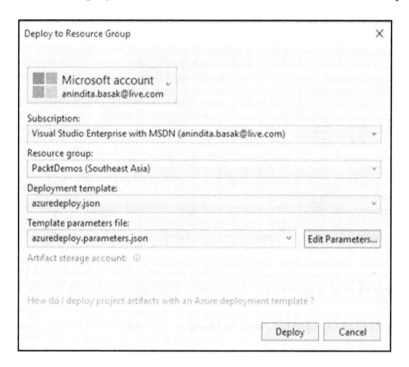

- Monitoring of Azure Stream Analytics job provisioning using ARM templates from VS:

```
Output
Show output from:  PacktDemos
20:13:50 - ResourceGroupName        : PacktDemos
20:13:50 - ProvisioningState        : Succeeded
20:13:50 - Timestamp                : 09/24/2017 2:43:49 PM
20:13:50 - Mode                     : Incremental
20:13:50 - TemplateLink             :
20:13:50 - TemplateLinkString       :
20:13:50 - DeploymentDebugLogLevel  :
20:13:50 - Parameters               : {[streamAnalyticsJobName,
20:13:50 -                            Microsoft.Azure.Commands.ResourceManager.Cmdlets.SdkModels.DeploymentVariable],
20:13:50 -                            [numberOfStreamingUnits,
20:13:50 -                            Microsoft.Azure.Commands.ResourceManager.Cmdlets.SdkModels.DeploymentVariable]}
20:13:50 - ParametersString         :
20:13:50 -                            Name                     Type                        Value
20:13:50 -                            ===============          ========================    ==========
20:13:50 -                            streamAnalyticsJobName   String                      packtasajob
20:13:50 -                            numberOfStreamingUnits   Int                         1
20:13:50 -
20:13:50 - Outputs                  :
20:13:50 - OutputsString            :
20:13:50 -
20:13:50 -
20:13:50 -
20:13:50 - Successfully deployed template 'azuredeploy.json' to resource group 'PacktDemos'.
```

Configuration of the Azure Streaming job with different input data sources and output data sinks

In real-time data analytics architecture pipelines, there's need for data ingestion from various sources, and similarly, the pushing out of the processed data to various sinks either for further stream processing, long-term archival perspective, or storing as a relational database level. Azure Stream Analytics, as a master product of Azure Interactive Data Analytics architecture, is not an exception to this. Stream Analytics provides various data ingestion layers as part of continuous data streams to be pushed into streaming jobs as Data Streams. The static data ingestion layer is to capture a slowly changed compound dataset as a Reference Data Stream.

In the output topology layer, a Stream Analytics job provides a seamless integration capability as the sink layer with Azure data resources like Azure SQL database, Blob storage, Table Storage, Service Bus topic, and Queues, the rich real-time visualization business intelligence tool Power BI, massive petabyte-scale big data Hadoop-level volume data storage, Azure Data Lake Store, and globally distributed massive scaling out capable multimodel database—Cosmos DB. These data sink resources can be selected from the same Azure subscription or from a different subscription that the respective account has access to.

Data input types-data stream and reference data

Stream Analytics provides support for Data Stream as a continuous unlimited sequence of events over a particular timestamp referenced by Azure Event Hub, IoT Hub, and Blob storage. A job should contain at least one data stream input, which contains complex events from any of a wide variety of data sources like vehicle sensors, devices, social feeds, and clickstreams.

The reference data is defined as static data blocks that have slow modification and schema updates. Azure Blob storage supports reference data stream sources for Stream Analytics jobs to perform mainly data correlation, joining, and lookups.

Data Stream inputs

- **Azure Event Hub**: Azure Service Bus, Event Hub is a real-time Publish/Subscribe stream ingestor component that has multipartitioning and a message retention capability of up to seven days by default. Each message gets stored in each partition block as the event ingestor model inside the Azure Event Hub, and a maximum of 32 partitioning units can be configured for the Event Hub. Complex streams of events from device to cloud push to Stream Analytics using Event Hub with a timestamp. Azure Blob storage can also be configured for the archival of processed data through the Event Hub. The Event Hub can be configured with claims like **listen, read,** and **send** using the **REST API**.

The configuration of Stream Analytics job topology input with Azure Event Hub as Data Stream input integration:

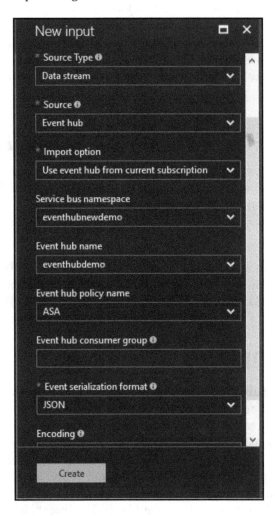

- **Azure IoT Hub**: This is a Publish/Subscriber data ingestor from real-world IoT devices, gateways, edge services, and sensors with bi-directional communication capabilities like device-to-cloud and cloud-to-device Event flows. Streams from IoT sensors and devices get processed through stream analytics using a timestamp an Event payload.
- **Azure Blob storage**: In case studies like weblog telemetry analysis, where a massive amount of unstructured, semi-structured, or quasi-structured data to be processed through Azure Stream Analytics, Blob storage is used as a Data Stream ingestor for ASA jobs in these scenarios. Events of petabyte volume big data are processed in real time using a timestamp.

Reference data

Azure Blob storage defines the capacity of stream ingestion static and auxiliary in nature into Stream Analytics as reference data. By default, reference data has a restriction of processing 100 MB per blob by ASA jobs and can ingest data from multiple reference data blobs at a time.

Job topology output data sinks of Stream Analytics

- **Azure SQL database**: The output of the Stream Analytics job is relational in nature with well-defined schema and can be hosted for applications such as RDBMS and can be stored as Azure SQL database tables. Schema queries of ASA jobs and DB-level column schema of Azure SQL DB must match.

Azure SQL data warehouse can also be configured as an output of ASA jobs, which is a petabyte-scale MPP solution.

- **Azure Table storage**: This helps store the output of ASA jobs, which are structured, key-value pairs with partitions but non-relational in nature. Azure Table storage is a highly available NoSQL key/value pair data model storage.
- **Power BI**: This is a rich set of visualization BI tools with great support for Azure and REST API to build near real-time, highly interactive charts, graphs, and events analysis. Stream Analytics jobs can be integrated with Microsoft Power BI using authentication and authorization through office 365 and Azure AD tenant. Make sure that you use the same account for Azure and office 365 integration.

- **Azure Cosmos DB**: This is a NoSQL key/value paired globally distributed massive scaling out the capable interactive database. The database ships with high availability and reliability through all Azure regions and maintains consistency in reading operations.
- **Azure Blob storage**: This is used to store processed streams in long-term archival or infrequent access level; ASA jobs can be integrated with Azure Blob storage as output. Files in blob storage are indexed by **Path Patterns**.
- **Azure Event Hub**: In scenarios like if the output streams of ASA job could be an input of another Streaming job, then Azure Service Bus Event Hub can be used as an output and could be ingested further as stream input for further stream processing.
- **Azure Service Bus queue and topic**: Service Bus queue as a **First-in-First-Out** (**FIFO**) data structure provides intercommunication between direct streaming jobs to message stores. Further, the messages could be published or subscribed based on the topic suggested in the Service Bus topic configuration. Service Bus topic, which provides one-to-many communication channels, can also be used as an output message sink of Stream Analytics jobs.
- **Azure Data Lake Store**: This offers petabyte-scale massive parallel data storage capability on the cloud with the Hadoop file system (web-HDFS) integration capability to process big data. While integrating Azure Data Lake Store as an output of Stream Analytics, it needs to be authorized to approve permanent level access to a Data Lake Store account as output.

Summary

In this chapter, we created a stream analytics job using Stream Analytics tools for Visual Studio. Through this application, we demonstrated how to test Stream Analytics jobs with local sample data in Visual Studio, testing queries locally, monitoring jobs, and publishing to Azure from the Visual Studio environment. We created a Stream Analytics job step by step using the Azure portal itself. Finally, we defined how to provision a streaming job in Azure using the ARM template with its various input and output data sink resources.

In the next chapter, we'll be focusing on the stream processing logic in Azure stream, expressed in SQL-like query language to perform transformation, aggregation, and computation over real-time streams of events.

5
Building Using Stream Analytics Query Language

In this chapter, we will explore the SQL-like query language used in Azure Stream Analytics to run transformations and computations on streaming data. We'll discuss how common and complex stream processing requirements can be met with straightforward queries, demonstrating with samples along the way.

Specifically, the topics we will cover in the chapter are:

- Using built-in functions within queries to parse, aggregate, and transform streaming data
- Working with simple and complex data types typical of streaming data
- Exploring the building block elements of the Stream Analytics query language
- Windowing to perform computation on events grouped by configurable periods of time
- Handling the temporal nature of streaming data with job configuration settings and time management query patterns
- Understanding event delivery guarantees offered by Stream Analytics

 Most examples in this chapter use data and resources generated by the Cortana Intelligence Gallery solution template Telemetry Analytics, available at https://gallery.cortanaintelligence.com/Solution/ Telemetry-Analytics.

Built-in functions

Stream Analytics query language (**SAQL**) comes with many built-in functions to assist with aggregating and transforming data. These functions can help us with simple operations on a single value, as in data type conversions and string concatenations, as well as with more complex operations, like identifying the first event in a period of time or geospatial intersections of event locations. Types of built-in functions include scalar, record, mathematical, input metadata, date and time, aggregate, analytic, geospatial, and array functions.

Scalar functions

Simple functions that operate on a single value and return a single value are known as **scalar functions**. SAQL provides many scalar functions for string manipulation. For example, UPPER capitalizes all characters in a string expression, as in the following query example:

```
select ehinput.timestamp, ehinput.vin, ehinput.speed,
ehinput.outsidetemperature,
    UPPER(ehinput.city) as city
from ehinput
```

Note the uppercase values in column **City**:

TIMESTAMP	VIN	SPEED	OUTSIDETEMPERATURE	CITY
"2017-10-12T16:55:14.23133...	"KW6NJBUOY58HB85HB"	42	60	"BELLEVUE"
"2017-10-12T16:55:13.55027...	"K91ACNEWB115DSZ6A"	77	71	"SEATTLE"
"2017-10-12T16:55:13.77561...	"N93EHZ8F1QX4RW0DU"	55	45	"SEATTLE"
"2017-10-12T16:55:14.00094...	"O8WNOB755ZBQMM4E0"	94	98	"REDMOND"
"2017-10-12T16:55:15.1442E...	"CIWU6VOE7047MO7NUE...	71	91	"BELLEVUE"

Additional scalar functions include, but are not limited to:

- **SUBSTRING**: To return a part of a string value, beginning with a given position number and extending a given length

    Syntax: `SUBSTRING (string_expression, start_position, length)`

- **CONCAT**: To concatenate two or more string values

    Syntax: `CONCAT (string_value1, string_value2[, string_valueN])`

    Example: CONCAT ('Bill', ' ', 'Gates')—returns 'Bill Gates'

- **LEN**: To return the length of a string expression

    Syntax: `LEN (string_expression)`

    Example: LEN ('Bill Gates')—returns 10

- **REGEXMATCH**: To return the position number of the first occurrence of a regular expression pattern within a given expression, or, if the regular expression pattern does not occur, return zero

    Syntax: `REGEXMATCH (expression, pattern)`

    Example: REGEXMATCH ('FWH4V0EZ017WL7NJH', '[0-9][0-9]')—returns 9

Aggregate and analytic functions

Aggregate functions perform calculations on a group of events and return a single event or value. Aggregate functions are deterministic, so given the same input, they will always return the same result. They can only be used in a projection (that is, a SELECT clause) or an aggregate constraint (that is, a HAVING clause). For example, `AVG` returns the average of values in a group.

The following example, based on an incoming stream of data from connected vehicles, shows average vehicle speed in each city, calculated per minute:

```
select System.Timestamp as WindowEndTimestamp, ehinput.city,
    AVG(ehinput.speed) as average_speed
from ehinput timestamp by ehinput.timestamp
group by ehinput.city, TumblingWindow(minute, 1)
```

The query results show one row per minute per city, with the average speed calculated:

WINDOWENDTIMESTAMP	CITY	AVERAGE_SPEED
"2017-10-12T16:56:00.0000000Z"	"Sammamish"	33.53846153846154
"2017-10-12T16:56:00.0000000Z"	"Seattle"	52.24193548387097
"2017-10-12T16:56:00.0000000Z"	"Bellevue"	67.63380281690141
"2017-10-12T16:56:00.0000000Z"	"Redmond"	57.97959183673469
"2017-10-12T16:57:00.0000000Z"	"Sammamish"	32.69230769230769
"2017-10-12T16:57:00.0000000Z"	"Seattle"	53.98837209302326

Among the other commonly used aggregate functions provided by SAQL are:

- **SUM**: To return the sum of a set of values

    Syntax: `SUM (expression)`

- **COUNT**: To return the number of items in a group

    Syntax: `COUNT (expression)`

- **MIN**: To return the minimum value in a given expression

    Syntax: `MIN (expression)`

- **MAX**: To return the maximum value in a given expression

    Syntax: `MAX (expression)`

- **COLLECT**: To return an array of events identified in a time window

    Syntax: `COLLECT ()`

The following example shows an array of events collected for each 30-second time window:

```
select COLLECT()
from ehinput timestamp by ehinput.timestamp
group by TumblingWindow(second, 30)
```

The preceding query output shows an array per row, with each array containing the events that occurred within each 30-second window. The . . . indicates the results display cannot fit the entire array:

COLLECT
[{"vin":"K91ACNEWB115DSZ6A","outsideTemperature":71,"engineTemperature":459,"speed":77,"fuel":37,"engineoil":36,"tirepressure":31,"odometer":148231,"...
[{"vin":"CI7HNL5Z8RQZBHH75","outsideTemperature":98,"engineTemperature":459,"speed":94,"fuel":26,"engineoil":49,"tirepressure":49,"odometer":127771,"...
[{"vin":"3GLUZWIHRNDSTQD4L","outsideTemperature":81,"engineTemperature":215,"speed":71,"fuel":17,"engineoil":41,"tirepressure":35,"odometer":148005,...
[{"vin":"B2C46I8SHH5Q08LUL","outsideTemperature":76,"engineTemperature":163,"speed":63,"fuel":19,"engineoil":38,"tirepressure":31,"odometer":160719,"ci...
[{"vin":"FDNLEQHWRHQGSS5GP","outsideTemperature":96,"engineTemperature":412,"speed":93,"fuel":10,"engineoil":48,"tirepressure":47,"odometer":166112...
[{"vin":"XGNRWZGZO3D9B3KGB","outsideTemperature":98,"engineTemperature":448,"speed":96,"fuel":2,"engineoil":49,"tirepressure":48,"odometer":72869,"c...

- **TopOne**: To return the first occurring event in an ordered set of events, where the ordering is defined by columns and the time window of the query

  Syntax: `TopOne () OVER (ORDER BY (column name1 [ASC|DESC] [, column name2 [ASC|DESC]])`

In the following example, `TopOne` is used to detect the fastest car in each city every minute:

```
select ehinput.city, System.Timestamp as WindowEndTimestamp,
    TopOne() OVER (ORDER BY ehinput.speed DESC) as Fastest
from ehinput timestamp by ehinput.timestamp
group by ehinput.city, TumblingWindow(minute, 1)
```

The output shows new column **FASTEST** with one record returned for each city each minute. The **FASTEST** column contains the event associated with the car speeding the fastest:

CITY	WINDOWENDTIMESTAMP	FASTEST
"Sammamish"	"2017-10-12T16:56:00.0000000Z"	{"vin":"0TRTC0ZNZP8VJY56Y","outsideTemperatur...
"Seattle"	"2017-10-12T16:56:00.0000000Z"	{"vin":"0XRQ73YKQYE8W2E37","outsideTemperat...
"Bellevue"	"2017-10-12T16:56:00.0000000Z"	{"vin":"05PWRS63RJZUO1W1K","outsideTemperat...
"Redmond"	"2017-10-12T16:56:00.0000000Z"	{"vin":"090365V7V4TLXXI1C","outsideTemperatur...
"Sammamish"	"2017-10-12T16:57:00.0000000Z"	{"vin":"20Q8Q0OL6VU1OZTS5","outsideTemperat...
"Seattle"	"2017-10-12T16:57:00.0000000Z"	{"vin":"0AIQACAOYU097SI8S","outsideTemperatu...

- **STDEV**: To return the standard deviation of all values in a group, ignoring null values

Syntax: `STDEV (expression)`

Analytic functions also aggregate events over a time window, but unlike aggregate functions, they can return multiple rows per group. Analytic functions can help compare events to other events within a group, enabling solutions to many typical **Internet of Things (IoT)** and streaming problems. For example, `ISFIRST` returns a Boolean 1 or 0, depending on whether a given condition was met for the first time within a given time window.

The following example indicates, for each city, the first time a car moved faster than 70 miles per hour. The city, unique vehicle identifier, timestamp, and exact speed are included in the results as well. Note that all the other events in the window are also returned in the query results, along with the indication that they were not the first to eclipse 70 miles per hour.

Following is the example query with `ISFIRST` used to compute an indicator value in a new column:

```
select ehinput.city, ehinput.timestamp, ehinput.vin, ehinput.speed,
    ISFIRST(mi, 10) OVER(PARTITION BY ehinput.city when ehinput.speed > 70)
as first_over_70
from ehinput
```

The output shows all records returned, with one vehicle flagged as the first car in **Redmond** during that 10-minute window to speed over 70 miles per hour:

CITY	TIMESTAMP	VIN	SPEED	FIRST_OVER_70
"Bellevue"	"2017-10-08T17:20:17.3349336Z"	"KYPJSRXSEEWS5C75P"	62	0
"Seattle"	"2017-10-08T17:20:17.1005500Z"	"A938JQWGD06NE5GJB"	65	0
"Seattle"	"2017-10-08T17:20:17.5724282Z"	"SPS2HK5GEOM4G8C1E"	67	0
"Seattle"	"2017-10-08T17:20:17.7911871Z"	"V2XCUCHXDBW83G0CN"	6	0
"Seattle"	"2017-10-08T17:20:18.2599469Z"	"6DP2D5TG3HMPV3OFE"	8	0
"Sammamish"	"2017-10-08T17:20:18.0255687Z"	"08SDUHPVLM4GZPXZ0"	33	0
"Sammamish"	"2017-10-08T17:20:18.5008015Z"	"HF4UKFMQ86SYX6V8D"	35	0
"Redmond"	"2017-10-08T17:20:18.7465626Z"	"KUPBVVXOPNHQFYBFF"	93	1

Other analytic functions provided by SAQL are:

- **LAST**: To look up the most recent event within a time window, which, optionally, meets a given condition

  Syntax: `LAST (expression[, default]) OVER ([PARTITION BY partition key] LIMIT DURATION(unit, length) [WHEN boolean expression])`

The following example shows, separately for each city, the unique identifier (`vin`) of the car that most recently speed over 70 miles per hour. The time window in this example is defined as the 24 hours leading to each event.

Following is the example query with `LAST` used to return the appropriate vehicle identification number, if any:

```
select ehinput.city, ehinput.timestamp, ehinput.vin, ehinput.speed,
    LAST(ehinput.vin) OVER(PARTITION BY ehinput.city limit duration(hour,
24) when ehinput.speed > 70) as last_car_over_70
from ehinput
```

The query output shows the most recent speeding car's **VIN** for each city within each 24-hour window. Note the result **null** for rows within a city's 24-hour period for which no car had speed preceding 70 miles per hour, at least not yet in that period:

CITY	TIMESTAMP	VIN	SPEED	LAST_CAR_OVER_70
"Bellevue"	"2017-10-08T17:20:17.3349336Z"	"KYPJSRXSEEWS5C75P"	62	null
"Redmond"	"2017-10-08T17:20:18.7465626Z"	"KUPBVVXOPNHQFYBFF"	93	"KUPBVVXOPNHQFYBFF"
"Redmond"	"2017-10-08T17:20:19.2140664Z"	"979MIDT0U635Z4MJ3"	95	"979MIDT0U635Z4MJ3"
"Redmond"	"2017-10-08T17:20:18.9779613Z"	"1NY9MI2JAR20A6799"	20	"979MIDT0U635Z4MJ3"
"Bellevue"	"2017-10-08T17:20:19.4387411Z"	"C3CZU059UKJTK52V3"	59	null
"Redmond"	"2017-10-08T17:20:20.1889220Z"	"60F6J6XRQMDX8YZGS"	20	"979MIDT0U635Z4MJ3"
"Bellevue"	"2017-10-08T17:20:19.9050540Z"	"HIY403UZ5QSU9D9T1"	92	"HIY403UZ5QSU9D9T1"
"Bellevue"	"2017-10-08T17:20:20.4197946Z"	"HCHAJQOQ1ZN19VN7W"	64	"HIY403UZ5QSU9D9T1"
"Redmond"	"2017-10-08T17:20:21.3373221Z"	"N8A454W2LQAAG8WNM"	11	"979MIDT0U635Z4MJ3"

- **LAG**: To return the immediately preceding event within a time window, which, optionally, meets a given condition

  Syntax: `LAG (expression[, offset] [, default]) OVER ([PARTITION BY partition key] LIMIT DURATION(unit, length) [WHEN boolean expression])`

The following example illustrates the use of `LAG` to look up values from previous events. In this example of vehicle events, `LAG` is used to look up the previous speed at which a car was moving. Previous speed is compared to the speed of the current event in order to calculate a change in speed.

Following is the example query with `LAG`:

```
select ehinput.vin, ehinput.city, ehinput.timestamp, ehinput.speed,
    ehinput.speed -
    LAG(ehinput.speed) OVER(PARTITION BY ehinput.city, ehinput.vin limit
duration(hour, 24)) as speed_change
from ehinput
```

The following output shows new column **SPEED_CHANGE**, which contains the results of the LAG comparison. Note that **null** is returned when there is no previous event for the same car in the same city within the same 24-hour period, for instance in the first record returned. Zero is returned when there are multiple events within these parameters, but no change in speed between the events, as seen in the second record from the bottom in the sample output. When there are multiple vehicle events in the same city and 24-hour period, then we can observe a non-zero value returned in the **SPEED_CHANGE** column, as in the bottom record:

VIN	CITY	TIMESTAMP	SPEED	SPEED CHANGE
"6DP2D5TG3HMPV3OFE"	"Seattle"	"2017-10-08T17:20:18.2599469Z"	8	null
"56H3FPUVHSKUOXFQS"	"Seattle"	"2017-10-08T17:20:47.3947682Z"	57	null
"4KSSG8Y4VNHOOM8V8"	"Seattle"	"2017-10-08T17:21:02.2275701Z"	8	null
"9DC3XI86623BSWVNO"	"Seattle"	"2017-10-08T17:21:31.6304570Z"	3	null
"6DP2D5TG3HMPV3OFE"	"Seattle"	"2017-10-08T17:21:58.3684600Z"	58	50
"9DC3XI86623BSWVNO"	"Seattle"	"2017-10-08T17:22:14.5609439Z"	60	57
"56H3FPUVHSKUOXFQS"	"Seattle"	"2017-10-08T17:23:12.6801248Z"	57	0
"4KSSG8Y4VNHOOM8V8"	"Seattle"	"2017-10-08T17:23:13.6117357Z"	72	64

Array functions

Arrays are used to store multiple values, and these are very often found in streaming data. For example, an office building conference room with one or more motion sensors could be represented with the help of an array:

```
{
    "id": "c84f7b5c-0da0-4832-ba53-7e40a00e579f",
    "conferenceRoom": "Market Research Lab",
    "sensors": [
        {
            "sensorId": "7d7785fe-6514-421a-9808-19594f47e96d"
        },
        {
```

```
        "sensorId": "a5fb1a3e-403a-4084-b0c6-7244efea1b63"
    }
  ]
}
```

We may need to count the number of motion sensors per conference room or to analyze motion activity associated with each individual sensor, or some other transformation or aggregation. Furthermore, arrays can be nested, creating a tree-like structure in a single string. Perhaps a *buildings* array would contain individual buildings, each with rooms in a *rooms* array, and each of those with sensors in a *sensors* array, as in our example. This array nesting potential and the variation in the number of elements per array (from one to many sensors, in our example) pose unique challenges for querying array data. To help with these challenges, SAQL provides specific functions to process and parse arrays, returning array elements and metadata.

The following example shows the sensors array, transformed by SAQL array function `GetArrayElement`. The function retrieves individual elements (sensors, in this case) by the zero-based index value, and puts them each in a separate column in the output.

Following is the example query with `GetArrayElement` used for each projected column:

```
select GetArrayElement(ehinput.sensors, 0) as firstSensor,
    GetArrayElement(ehinput.sensors, 1) as secondSensor
from ehinput
```

The following query output shows the data for each motion sensor in its own column:

FIRSTSENSOR	SECONDSENSOR
{"sensorId":"59ffef02-8d6d-4a2d-a603-d16d06a0e903"}	{"sensorId":"4180326f-7fcb-4372-9918-d0ec5a90dc08"}

Other array functions are:

- `GetArrayLength`: To return the number of elements in an array

    Syntax: `GetArrayLength (array expression)`

The following example counts the motion sensors in each conference room message. Following is the example query with `GetArrayLength` used to count the length of the sensors array:

```
select ehinput.conferenceRoom,
    GetArrayLength(ehinput.sensors) as countOfMotionSensors
from ehinput
```

The following output shows a single record for conference room **Market Research Lab** and 2 sensors:

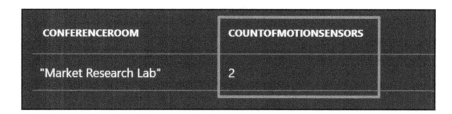

CONFERENCEROOM	COUNTOFMOTIONSENSORS
"Market Research Lab"	2

- `GetArrayElements`: To return array indexes and values in a dataset; the results must be used with the `CROSS APPLY` operator

Syntax: `GetArrayLength (array expression)`

The following example shows the array elements of conference room motion sensors separated into rows in the output. The example query shows `GetArrayElements` used to return the index and values inside an array:

```
select ehinput.conferenceRoom,
    arrayElement.arrayIndex as sensorIndex,
    arrayElement.arrayValue as sensorValue
from ehinput
CROSS APPLY GetArrayElements(ehinput.sensors) as arrayElement
```

The output for the example query shows the zero-based index for the array elements and the value from the array in its own column:

CONFERENCEROOM	SENSORINDEX	SENSORVALUE
"Market Research Lab"	0	{"sensorId":"59ffef02-8d6d-4a2d-a603-d16d06a0e903"}
"Market Research Lab"	1	{"sensorId":"4180326f-7fcb-4372-9918-d0ec5a90dc08"}

Other functions

SAQL provides many other built-in functions to assist with a wide variety of computation scenarios. Other handy functions include geospatial functions for reading and writing geospatial data structures, an input metadata function to look up properties of the data source, conversion functions to change or work with data types, and mathematical functions to perform deterministic calculations on input values.

Following is a selection of other common and important SAQL functions:

- `CreatePoint`: To return a GeoJSON point record, including a coordinates array. The result can be used for other geospatial functions

  Syntax: `CreatePoint (latitude, longitude)`

  Example: CreatePoint (3.0, -10.2) returns {"type" : "Point", "coordinates" : [-10.2, 3.0]}

- `ST_DISTANCE`: To return the distance in meters between two points

  Syntax: `ST_DISTANCE (pointFrom, pointTo)`

  Example: ST_DISTANCE (CreatePoint (-5.0, -5.0), CreatePoint (0.0, 0.0)) returns 784028.74077501823

- `FLOOR`: To return, from the input, the largest integer that is no greater than the given expression

  Syntax: `FLOOR (expression)`

- `TRY_CAST`: To return a value whose data type is converted to the given data type if possible; returning null if not possible

  Syntax: `TRY_CAST (expression as data_type)`

Data types and formats

Every data value processed by Stream Analytics, whether from an incoming or outgoing data stream, set of reference data or computed in an expression, is classified as a particular data type. Data types define which values can be held in a column or expression. Stream Analytics supports the data types bigint, float, nvarchar (max), datetime, record, and array.

Currently, the serialization formats compatible with Stream Analytics are CSV, JSON, and Avro. While CSV data has a simple structure, JSON and Avro can contain complex structures.

Complex types

As previously discussed, arrays are a complex data type posing unique query processing challenges. In our sensors example, a series of motion sensors are contained in an array within a conference room, which itself is one in a series of rooms contained in an array within an office building, which is in a series of buildings in an array. This nested array of sensors within rooms within buildings is a complex structure, all contained in a single column or expression, usually defined with either the Array or Record data types.

Following is a sample of one conference room:

```
{
    "id": "ba5fbde4-bfa1-4046-b361-7dd27019a55f",
    "conferenceRoom": "Market Research Lab",
    "readings":
    {
        "Temperature" : 71,
        "Humidity" : 52,
        "Pressure" : 22
    }
}
```

The Array data type defines an ordered collection of values. We have seen the operations that can be run on arrays with SAQL array functions GetArrayElement, GetArrayLength, and GetArrayElements.

The Record data type in SAQL represents streaming JSON and Avro arrays. The Record type enables techniques to treat complex types as a simple structure.

In the following example, the temperature is accessed from the (sensor) readings array:

```
select conferenceRoom,
    readings.temperature
from ehinput
```

The output for the query shows the row-based structure produced by SAQL, with temperature as its own column:

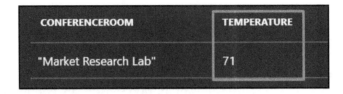

The familiar * can be used to access all elements in an array without explicitly naming each element. The below query returns all elements from the readings array:

```
select conferenceRoom,
    readings.*
from ehinput
```

Observe that the readings array elements have been transformed into columns in the produced output:

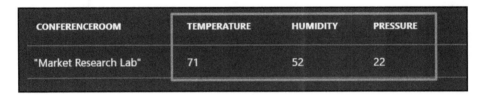

Query language elements

Many of the familiar building blocks of SQL queries are also provided by SAQL. A few of the most common and fundamental elements are:

- SELECT, for projecting columns in the query output
- FROM, for setting the input or input-derived data source
- CASE, for condition evaluation
- WHERE, for filtering input data

Certain other SAQL elements, while familiar from traditional database query patterns, have distinctive benefits for streaming data. Let's take a closer look at a few of them:

- **WITH**: Defines a temporary derived table for later reference in the query. That much is the well-known role that WITH plays in SQL, but in Stream Analytics, it also helps when scaling out a query for more efficient handling of a higher throughput workload. Because the result set defined by WITH can be referenced multiple times in the query, encapsulating common business logic there can yield significant savings in the resources used by the Stream Analytics job.

  Syntax: `WITH result set alias1 AS (SELECT...) [, result set alias2 AS (SELECT...) [, result set aliasN AS (SELECT...)]]`

The following example shows WITH used to identify speeding activity from a vehicle event stream. The speeding activity is then referenced for multiple distinct output purposes, one for capturing all speeding and one for counting the number of speeding cars every ten minutes per city:

```
WITH Speeding AS
(
select *
from eventhubsource
where speed > 70
)

select city, vin, timestamp, speed
into AllSpeeding
from Speeding

select city, count(vin) as speedsters
into SpeedstersByCity
from Speeding
```

Observe the output from the first `select` showing `city`, `vin`, `timestamp`, and `speed` for all speeding events. Non-speeding events are ignored:

The output from the second `select` shows one row per city with a count of speeding cars. Non-speeding cars are not counted:

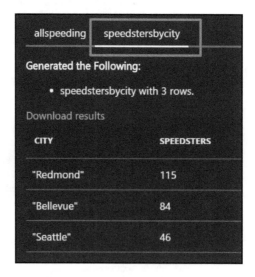

- **JOIN** integrates two or more inputs or input-derived data sets, just as it does in SQL. However, for Stream Analytics to integrate streaming data, JOIN requires the data sources to be temporally constrained. That is, we must match the sources for a window of time. JOIN requires the streaming sources to have temporal bounds defined, in order to avoid unbounded and unending record matches and so allow the query to complete and produce the output.

  > Syntax: `FROM input source1 [LEFT OUTER] JOIN input source2 ON DATEDIFF join condition [, result set alias2 AS (SELECT...) [, result set aliasN AS (SELECT...)]]`

The following example shows `JOIN` used to combine two streaming sources based on a window of time. The example shows instances when a car was observed in `Redmond` and in `Seattle` within ten minutes. The query uses `JOIN`, with the join condition based on a time window and being applied to both streaming sources `Redmond` and `Seattle`:

```
with
Redmond as
(select * from EventHubSource timestamp by eventhubsource.timestamp where
city = 'Redmond'),
Seattle as
(select * from EventHubSource timestamp by eventhubsource.timestamp where
city = 'Seattle')

select Redmond.vin as vin1, Seattle.vin as vin2
from Redmond
JOIN Seattle
ON Redmond.vin = Seattle.vin
and DATEDIFF(mi, Redmond, Seattle) between 0 and 10
```

- **Reference Data JOIN** is a specialized join in Stream Analytics. Often an event stream needs to be combined with more static data, or reference data, to get real insight. Reference data sources are integrated with Stream Analytics queries to meet a variety of needs. Real-time alarm triggering is often dependent on alarm thresholds being maintained in a reference dataset outside of Stream Analytics. Incoming data can also be enriched with business-friendly descriptions from reference data. Note that a real-time capability may also be maintained with this technique by obviating the need for downstream processing to enrich the data after the Stream Analytics job completes.

In the following example, the streaming input `EventHubSource` contains vehicle events but does not include the vehicle model in its payload. Model is maintained in a reference data set in Blob storage and used in the query as `BlobSource`. By joining the streaming `EventHubSource` to the reference data `BlobSource`, we can include a `Model` column in the query output.

Following is the query with a Reference Data `JOIN`:

```
select EventHubSource.vin, BlobSource.Model, EventHubSource.timestamp,
EventHubSource.outsideTemperature
into EventHubOut
from EventHubSource
JOIN BlobSource on EventHubSource.vin = BlobSource.VIN
```

Windowing

Continuously streaming data makes real-time computations and insights possible, overcoming the latency inherent in batch data processing systems. However, insights requiring aggregations of data, even very recent trending (for example, in the past 10 seconds), need to break the data stream into bounded groups of events. Time is a fundamental concept of streaming data systems and the natural construct to use when defining event boundaries for computing aggregations.

The following screenshot shows an event stream with defined time windows overlayed and sample computations produced. Note that the time windowing is fundamental to computing aggregates, like a count of events:

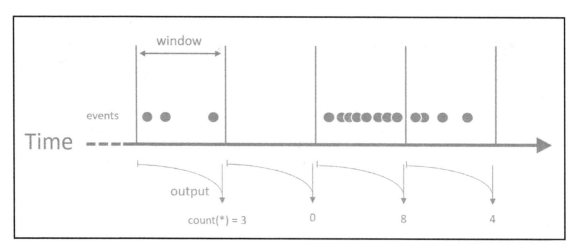

Stream Analytics uses windows of time to group events and supports window types that enable a variety of common event grouping patterns. In this section, we will examine the tumbling window, hopping window, and sliding window types. Stream Analytics windows are always used in the GROUP BY query clause. Queries will output the aggregated data at the end of the defined time window.

Tumbling windows

Tumbling windows are intervals defined to group events for aggregation. Tumbling windows are contiguous and of equal duration. They help with calculations on simple, regular intervals of time.

The following screenshot shows tumbling windows overlaid on an event stream:

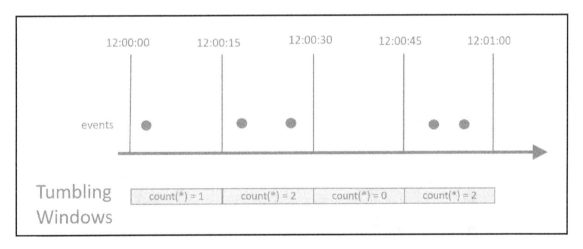

The following example shows average speed and count of cars per city for every ten seconds. A tumbling window of contiguous ten-second intervals is used to group the events for aggregations.

The following example query applies `TumblingWindow` to apply calculations to 10-second intervals:

```
select System.Timestamp as WindowEndTimestamp, ehinput.city,
    avg(ehinput.speed) as average_speed,
    count(ehinput.vin) as count_of_cars
from ehinput timestamp by ehinput.timestamp
group by ehinput.city, TumblingWindow(second, 10)
```

The output for the preceding query is as follows:

WINDOWENDTIMESTAMP	CITY	AVERAGE_SPEED	COUNT_OF_CARS
"2017-10-08T17:20:20.0000000Z"	"Sammamish"	34	2
"2017-10-08T17:20:20.0000000Z"	"Seattle"	41.8	5
"2017-10-08T17:20:20.0000000Z"	"Bellevue"	71	3
"2017-10-08T17:20:20.0000000Z"	"Redmond"	69.33333333333333	3
"2017-10-08T17:20:30.0000000Z"	"Sammamish"	36	1
"2017-10-08T17:20:30.0000000Z"	"Seattle"	55.5	12
"2017-10-08T17:20:30.0000000Z"	"Bellevue"	63.875	16
"2017-10-08T17:20:30.0000000Z"	"Redmond"	56.90909090909091	11

Hopping windows

Hopping windows group events for aggregation. Hopping windows are equal in duration but overlap at regular intervals. They can help with regular calculations where the time basis for aggregation is different from the frequency at which the calculation should be performed.

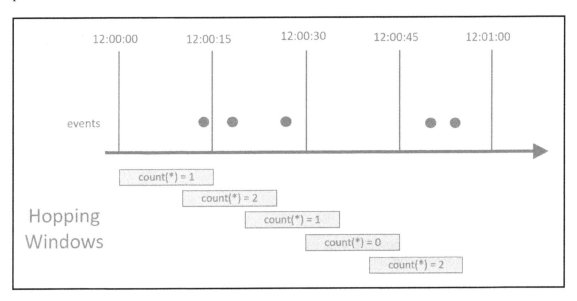

The following example shows the average speed and count of cars per city computed every two seconds but aggregated for the past ten seconds with each computation. In the following example query, a hopping window of overlapping ten-second intervals is used to group the events, with a new window starting every two seconds:

```
select System.Timestamp as WindowEndTimestamp, ehinput.city,
    avg(ehinput.speed) as average_speed,
    count(ehinput.vin) as count_of_cars
from ehinput timestamp by ehinput.timestamp
group by ehinput.city, HoppingWindow(Duration(second, 10), Hop(second, 2))
```

The output for the preceding query is as follows:

WINDOWENDTIMESTAMP	CITY	AVERAGE_SPEED	COUNT_OF_CARS
"2017-10-08T17:20:18.0000000Z"	"Seattle"	46	3
"2017-10-08T17:20:18.0000000Z"	"Bellevue"	62	1
"2017-10-08T17:20:20.0000000Z"	"Sammamish"	34	2
"2017-10-08T17:20:20.0000000Z"	"Seattle"	41.8	5
"2017-10-08T17:20:20.0000000Z"	"Bellevue"	71	3
"2017-10-08T17:20:20.0000000Z"	"Redmond"	69.33333333333333	3
"2017-10-08T17:20:22.00000007"	"Sammamish"	34.6666666666666664	3

Sliding windows

Sliding windows define all possible intervals of equal duration and output aggregations based on actual event stream activity. Sliding windows can be helpful when an event stream has unpredictable or spiky volume activity. They can help reduce the output during periods of inactivity or when the aggregation results remain unchanged.

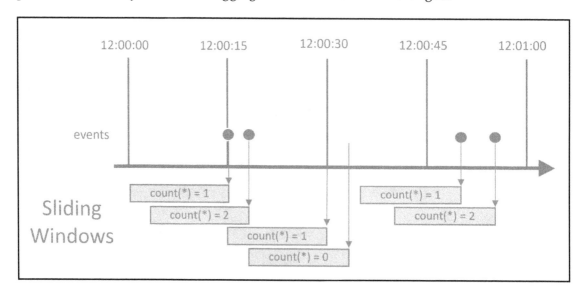

The following example shows the average speed and count of cars per city. The aggregates run over every 10-second window and return records every time a computation result changes. When a new car appears, a new record with 10-second computations is produced, with the car count incremented by one. Furthermore, when a car *stops* sending events for more than ten seconds, a new record with 10-second computations is also produced in this case, with the car count *decremented* by one.

Following is an example query with `SlidingWindow`:

```
select System.Timestamp as WindowEndTimestamp, ehinput.city,
    avg(ehinput.speed) as average_speed,
    count(ehinput.vin) as count_of_cars
from ehinput timestamp by ehinput.timestamp
group by ehinput.city, SlidingWindow(second, 10)
```

The output for the preceding query is as follows:

WINDOWENDTIMESTAMP	CITY	AVERAGE_SPEED	COUNT_OF_CARS
"2017-10-08T17:20:17.1005500Z"	"Seattle"	65	1
"2017-10-08T17:20:17.3349336Z"	"Bellevue"	62	1
"2017-10-08T17:20:17.5724282Z"	"Seattle"	66	2
"2017-10-08T17:20:17.7911871Z"	"Seattle"	46	3
"2017-10-08T17:20:18.0255687Z"	"Sammamish"	33	1
"2017-10-08T17:20:18.2599469Z"	"Seattle"	36.5	4
"2017-10-08T17:20:18.5008015Z"	"Sammamish"	34	2
"2017-10-08T17:20:18.7465626Z"	"Redmond"	93	1

The output shows irregular time windows in the records produced, as they are driven by actual event activity. Note that **Seattle** has four records produced in less than two seconds, each with rolling 10-second aggregate values, whereas **Sammamish** has just two records produced, and **Bellevue** and **Redmond** just have one each. That is due to actual vehicle activity in Seattle, Sammamish, Bellevue, and Redmond, and Seattle is evidently the busiest for the couple seconds.

Time management and event delivery guarantees

Windowing is an important query language extension that Stream Analytics provides to group events by time intervals, enabling aggregations of data streams. Other language extensions help with additional temporal aspects of stream data processing, including the source of the timestamp on which windows will be calculated, and the settings governing potential timestamp conflicts.

In a streaming system, a timestamp is the most fundamental data element in an event, and thus every event must have one in order to be processed or queried. In a simple streaming system, we can guarantee this by defining the moment each event arrives in the event stream as its identifying timestamp. (For Stream Analytics, the event stream is either Event Hub or IoT Hub.) Arrival Time is the default identifying timestamp of events. However, Stream Analytics provides a mechanism to choose a timestamp, known as Application Time, based on a column in the payload instead. Furthermore, we can reset the chosen timestamp from one query to the next.

`System.Timestamp` is the system property used to reference the identifying timestamp of an event in a query. If left to default, `System.Timestamp` represents Arrival Time. Otherwise, it represents Application Time.

The following example shows the event timestamp set to Application Time, based on column `ehinput.timestamp`:

```
select System.Timestamp as event_timestamp,
    ehinput.city,
    ehinput.speed
from ehinput timestamp by ehinput.timestamp
```

The output for the preceding query is as follows:

EVENT_TIMESTAMP	CITY	SPEED
"2017-10-08T17:20:17.1005500Z"	"Seattle"	65
"2017-10-08T17:20:17.3349336Z"	"Bellevue"	62
"2017-10-08T17:20:17.5724282Z"	"Seattle"	67
"2017-10-08T17:20:17.7911871Z"	"Seattle"	6
"2017-10-08T17:20:18.02556877"	"Sammamish"	33

When aggregating with a GROUP BY clause, the output event's timestamp is the end of the time window. For example, if windowing is defined by ten-second tumbling windows, then each resulting output event will be timestamped with the end of its ten-second window.

Application Time (from a column in the event payload) is typically a better representative of the real-world event than Arrival Time (when the record arrives in Event Hub or IoT Hub). Therefore, when a reliable timestamp is available in the event data, Application Time is usually chosen over Arrival Time. Stream Analytics sets Application Time by using the TIMESTAMP BY clause with the chosen timestamp column. Any payload column with a timestamp data type can be used.

In this example, Application Time is set with TIMESTAMP BY and the chosen payload column ehinput.timestamp:

```
select System.Timestamp as event_timestamp,
    ehinput.city,
    ehinput.speed
from ehinput timestamp by ehinput.timestamp
```

While Application Time is often the best representative of when an event actually occurred, depending on an externally generated value introduces a potential for conflicts with the streaming system. For example, events can arrive out of order or late, in terms of an Application Time. One common cause is related to scenarios where the events originate from not one but many external systems and those systems have conflicting clocks.

Event generating systems cease sending events to the streaming system at times, due to network disconnection for a period of time. When connectivity is restored, the buffered events would be sent to the streaming system, but in this case late as compared to events from continuously connected systems. Stream Analytics offers configurable policies to automatically manage the job's behavior in these circumstances.

The **Out of order events** policy defines a time allowance for events arriving out of order in the Stream Analytics job. It governs how long the Stream Analytics job would buffer events and, within that grace period, corrects the order according to the event timestamp set in the query. While the Out of order events policy is a helpful mechanism to manage timing conflicts, it does introduce latency equal to the time allowance duration itself.

Because by definition the job must buffer and wait for the amount of time set in the policy (three seconds in the following example), the query output is delayed by the same duration.

The following screenshot shows the Azure portal screen where the **Out of order events** policy is configured:

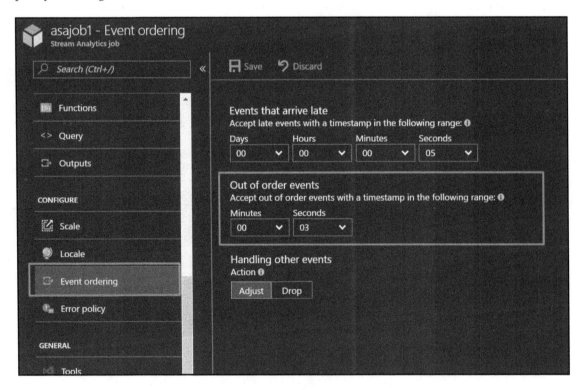

The **Late Arrival** policy defines a time allowance for events arriving late to Event Hub or IoT Hub. An event is late by the amount of time difference from the event timestamp to the input source timestamp; for example, Event Hub's enqueued time. The duration set in this policy is the maximum delay to accept late events. An event arriving with a timestamp older than this would be ignored by the Stream Analytics job.

The following screenshot shows the Azure portal screen where the late arrival policy is configured:

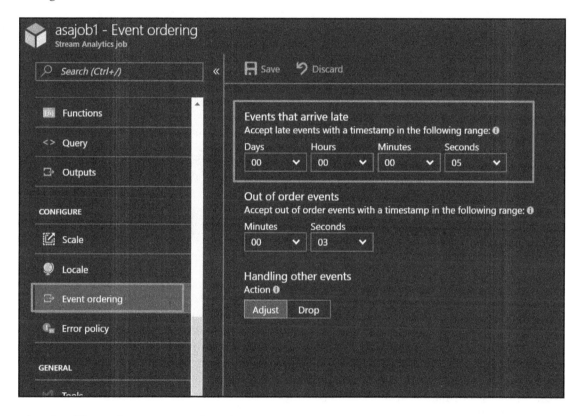

The **Handling other events** policy determines what action to take on events arriving outside the time allowances set in the Out of order and late arrival policies, whether to ignore the events or process them with adjusted timestamps.

The following screenshot shows the Azure portal screen where the **Handling other events** policy is configured:

Let's take an example where Application Time is 13:00:00, Arrival Time is 13:05:00, and the late arrival events policy is set to 1 minute. If the Handling other events policy is set to Adjust, Stream Analytics would adjust the event timestamp to 13:04:00. The query would process normally with the adjusted timestamp. The late arrival events policy determines that Application Time cannot be more than 1 minute behind Arrival Time. Therefore, at 13:05:00 Arrival Time, the System.Timestamp value gets adjusted to the oldest allowed timestamp of 1 minute behind, which is 13:04:00. On the other hand, if the Handling other events policy is set to Drop, then this event would be ignored altogether, and the query would process normally but without this event.

When the Handling other events policy is set to Adjust, Stream Analytics adjusts System.Timestamp based on the Late arrival policy first, and then applies the Out of order events policy next.

Summary

In this chapter, we explored the SQL-like Stream Analytics query language. We tried a wide variety of transformations using standard built-in functions, like substring and concatenation. We also used aggregate functions like sum, min, max, and count, and analytic functions for aggregating subsets of groups and comparing events to each other with first and lag. We worked with complex data types, parsing arrays and nested arrays, and reshaping them into a structured output. We then grouped events by windows of time for computing aggregates. Finally, we examined the time management policies used in Stream Analytics jobs to handle time-skewed events in streams. These SAQL techniques can be applied to enable the vast majority of streaming scenarios.

Now that we understand how to develop and implement SAQL query logic, in the next chapter, we will turn to scalability. We will learn about operationalizing Stream Analytics workloads from low to massive scales.

6

How to achieve Seamless Scalability with Automation

In the previous chapters, we looked into designing and developing on Azure Stream Analytics, constructing and querying real-time events from Azure Stream Analytics. This chapter we will take a detailed review of how to build, configure and deployment scalable streaming solution, improve query performance and a brief look at the deployment of Azure Stream Analytics.

Following is the list topics covered in this session:

- Understanding parts of Stream Analytics job definitions
- Deployment of Azure Stream Analytics using **Azure Resource Manager** (**ARM**)
- Vertical partitioning and horizontal partitioning to increase query performance
- Processing Out of order and late-arriving events

Understanding parts of a Stream Analytics job definition (input, output, reference data, and job)

Stream Analytics job definition includes inputs, a query, and output. We will start the topic with a brief introduction to input, output and query. We will look into each of the components in detail as follows:

- **Input**: Data connections to Stream Analytics from a given event source is called an **input**. For instance, Stream Analytics can connect directly to Azure Event Hubs, IoT Hub, and Blob storage to receive events. Do note that the Azure resource mentioned can be from the same or different subscriptions. Stream Analytics can handle high event throughput of up to 1 GB per second.
- **Reference data**: In addition to input, stream sets also support the second type of input, called auxiliary input (Reference data), to include a reference or static data.
- **Output**: Results sets from Stream Analytics are known as **output** and these can be written to various output devices such as Azure SQL DB, Event Hub, Table, Blob storage, Azure Service Bus topics or queues, and Power BI.
- **Query**: The query is used to transform the data input stream and generate output.
- **Job**: It requires at least one input source for data streaming. A job requires at least one input source for data streaming.

Stream Analytics connects directly to Azure Event Hubs for stream ingestion and the Azure Blob service to ingest historical data and take in millions of events per second. The data connection to Stream Analytics is a data stream of events from a data source.

The input sources are as follows:

Input source	Subscription scope
Azure Event Hub	Current subscription as your analytics job or a different subscription
Azure IoT Hub	Current subscription as your analytics job or a different subscription
Azure Blob storage	Current subscription as your analytics job or a different subscription

The input types are as follows:

Input type	Description	Compression
Data stream inputs	A constant stream of data that can be new feeds, IoT devices that collect data from devices, or log files.	Compression of all data stream input sources (Event Hubs, IoT Hub, and Blob storage). Supported Compression type is none, GZip, and Deflate compression.
Reference data	Any static data or data that changes very slowly is called **reference data**.	None

The output types are as follows:

Storage Type	Description	Security
Blob storage	Blob storage can be used for long-term archiving of the results.	The name of the storage account where you are sending your output to the Storage Account Key.
Table storage	Type of Key-Value pair data store; it can scale exponentially and automatically based on demand. Azure Table storage is a scalable NoSQL data store that enables you to store large volumes of semi-structured, non-relational data. It does not allow you to do complex joins, use foreign keys, or execute stored procedures. Each table has a single clustered index that can be used to query the data quickly.	Access key of the storage account where you are sending your output.
SQL database (Do note that an SQL server on IaaS is not supported)	Database table in SQL Azure where data will be written.	The username that has access to write to the database. The password to connect to the database.
Azure Data Lake Store as Service	This hyper-scale storage system can store data of any size with massive ingestion speed and an application agnostic storage service. Protects customers' future needs (data formats, volumes, processing paradigms, and consumers).	Authorizes an Azure Data Lake Store.
Event Hub	Scalable Pub/Sub data ingestion can collect millions of events in a given second. Event Hubs acts as the entry point for an event pipeline. Data can be stored and transformed once it's collected, stored, and transformed using any real-time analytics provider or batching/storage adapter.	Combination of **shared access signature** (SAS) tokens and event publishers.
Power BI	Results will be displayed in rich UI format for operational and dashboard functions.	Power BI user that can authorize access to Power BI.
Cosmos DB	Multi-modal databases with global distribution-offers a limitless elastic scale.	Cosmos DB account shared access key.
Azure Functions (Preview)	Serverless compute service to run code-on-demanded without any need to explicitly provision or de-provision the service. Can be invoked by Triggers from Azure or third party services.	Azure Function Key
Service Bus Topics	Use for one-to-many communication scenario	**Shared access signature (SAS)**
Service Bus Queues	Azure Queues provide at-least-once semantics in which each message may be read one or more times. This makes it important that all processing of the message be idempotent, which means the outcome of the processing must be the same regardless of how many times the message is processed. **First-in-first-out** (FIFO) is used for one-one communication. Only one consumer will consume the message.	Shared access signature

You cannot update credentials/keys on input/output while the job is running; the job needs to be stopped before the values can be updated. Azure Stream Analytics doesn't support resuming the job from the last know point.

The primary role of Event Hub is to provide a robust ingestion capability for incoming data that is being generated at data source endpoints such as devices or sensors. Once these events are loaded, the real-time event processing engine can then consume these events from Event Hub for performing temporal analytics.

Event Hub also provides storage entry point to robustly ingest data for short-term storage and can scale up to support large volumes of input and output events.

Event Hub from ground up is build to handle scale. We should understand a couple of key concepts on how the scale is handled in Event Hubs and it correlated to Azure Stream Analytics scaling architecture.

Following is the common event flow pattern and we have reviewed this in the earlier chapter:

Event flow pattern

Event publisher will publish data from a source event and will have hashed value known a partition key assigned by the sender for common data elements. Based on the partition key, event data is assigned to unique partitions within Event Hub. In order words, the data with the same partition keys get assigned to the same partition in Event Hub. One key consideration related to partition is availability, if you explicitly state the usage of partition key, then Azure will host separate node, in a situation if the node is not available there will be the delay in processing.

If you don't specify partition key, Azure will manage the availability and will host nodes in highlight resilient fashion and will use round-robin mechanism to distribute the message. This will result in data getting assigned randomly across the partitions:

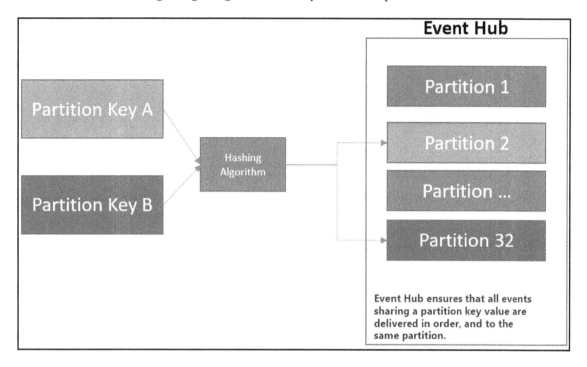

Partition Hashing logic

Currently, in Azure, a single Event Hub can have between 2 to 32 partitions. Do note, partitions are assigned during the deployed time and cannot be changed once Event Hub gets deployed. In this following example, we are configuring 32 partitions with 7 days data retention period. Currently, Event Hub supports 32 and it can change, so it's better to check the quotas regularly `https://docs.microsoft.com/en-us/azure/event-hubs/event-hubs-quotas`.

Configure Event Hub to handle scale

In streaming analytics scenario, the Event Hub can fulfill two separate roles as input and output sync. In the following design there are 3 distinct functions Data Ingest (Event Hub), Prepare and analyze (Azure Stream Analytics) and publish and consume (this can be different type including Event Hub). In the next session, we will we will deploy the Azure Stream Analytics using **Azure Resource Manager** (**ARM**) templates.

Deployment of Azure Stream Analytics using ARM template

Azure Stream Analytics ships with a pre-built adapter for Event Hubs, which significantly reduces the time to market for delivering solutions since developers do not need to develop their own custom adapters for the streaming engine. Additionally, and perhaps more significant for enabling accelerated solution deployment, Azure Stream Analytics provides a SQL-like language that allows database developers with existing SQL skills to transition to this platform very quickly. This language is very similar to T-SQL, which is the primary database language for SQL Server. However, it contains a superset of functions that support temporal operations such as applying sliding, hopping or tumbling time windows to the event stream.

The end goal of this section is an introduction to the deployment of Azure Stream Analytics ARM templates. Let's start with typical event ingest pattern using Azure Stream Analytics:

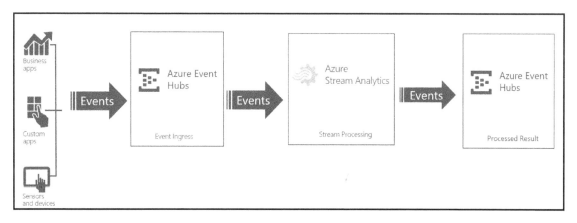

Creating an Event Hub and connecting it to Azure Stream Analytics using an ARM template

In this section, we will create an Event Hub and connect it to Azure Stream Analytics. For this example, we will use pre-built ARM templates that are available in the Microsoft Azure GitHub library to deploy Event Ingest Pattern with Event Hub and Azure Stream Analytics.

Follow the steps to deploy Event Hub and Integrate with Azure Stream Analytics :

1. Navigate to Quick start templates `https://github.com/Azure/azure-quickstart-templates`.
2. Look for **301-eventHub-create-authrule-namespace-and-eventHub/**:

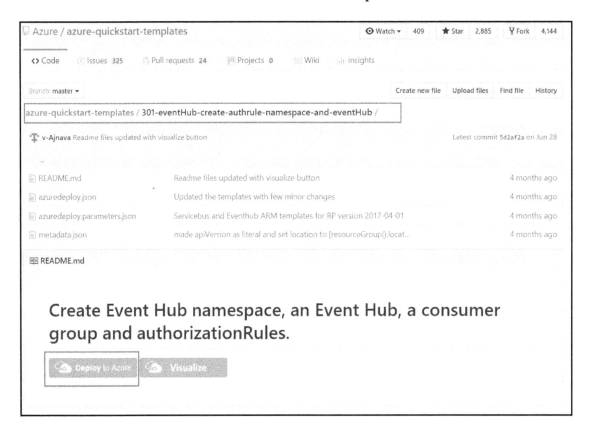

3. Provide the **Namespace** and **Event Hub Name**. Click on **Purchase**:

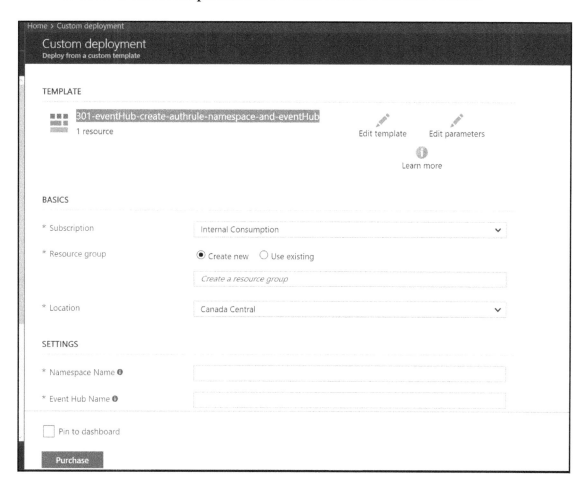

4. Then, Azure will start deploying Event Hub:

5. Once the deployment is complete, navigate to the resource:

Deploying Azure Stream Analytics

6. Navigate to `https://github.com/Azure/azure-quickstart-templates` and look
   for **101-streamanalytics-create/**:

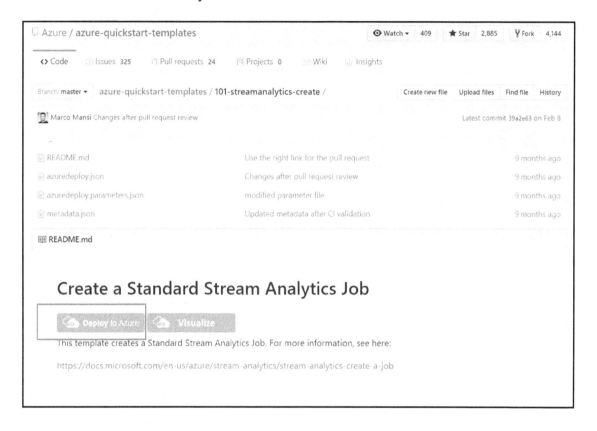

7. Configure the Stream Analytics with the appropriate values:

8. Azure will start deploying Azure Stream Analytics jobs:

9. Finally, the deployment process is complete:

10. Review the deployed Azure Stream Analytics job:

Configuring input

As we reviewed earlier in the canonical model, inputs can be configured from a number of sources in this example we will configure Event Hub as input source to receive input events. The ability of the Event Hub service to scale consumption elastically is important for real-time ingestion where the rate of incoming data streams can vary dramatically:

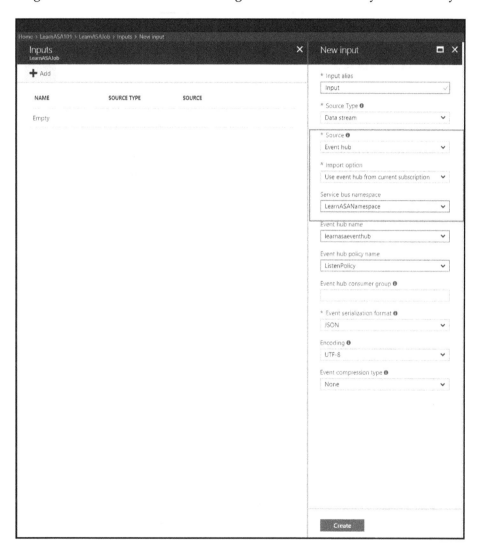

Once the input is configured and deployed, you will receive the following notification:

Configuring output

Azure stream analytics provides varieties of an option as output sink. In our example, we will use Event Hub as the output storage option for the processed data. Follow the steps to configure Event Hub as output sink:

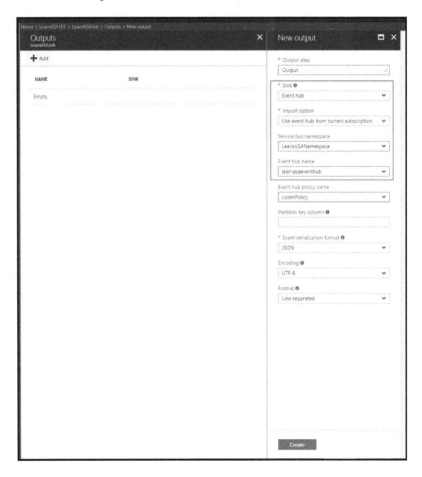

Once the output is configured and deployed, you will receive the following notification:

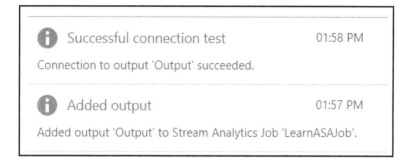

Building the sample test code

Once we have configured input and output, it can be tested with the following steps:

1. Navigate to **Inputs**, right-click, and choose **Sample Data** to test the input:

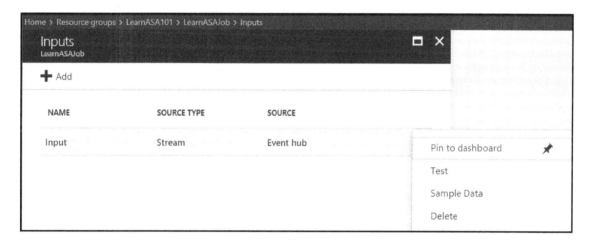

2. To build queries, after configuring the Input data, navigate to the main blade and click on **Query** in **JOB TOPOLOGY**:

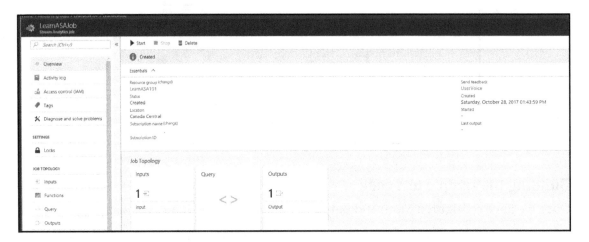

3. In the **Query** portal, you can build SQL-like queries to extract data from the input and push it to the output:

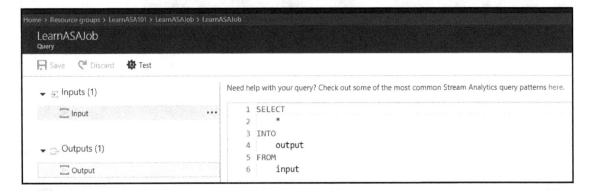

To summarize, in this section we looked into creating input, output, and also how to build simple queries. In the next section, we will look into how to build vertical and horizontal partitions to scale up the queries for faster performance.

How to scale queries using Streaming units and partitions

In traditional static data scenarios, the query can be executed against a fixed data set and results will be available after a known interval. On the other hand, with streaming data scenario involving constant changes to a dataset, the queries will run longer duration or might not even complete.

Additionally, a constant stream of data will increase the volume of data and query will drain the working memory. One way to draw data boundary is through the context of time. For example with streaming dataset, we can specify a data boundary that resides within the start and ends time. This will restrict the query execution between a known boundary. Application and arrival time are the two type of timing constraints we can use to set time boundaries for the streaming data.

Application and Arrival Time

Time at the event origin is known as the Application Time, time at event landing is called the Arrival Time. Within the queries, we can use TIMESTAMP BY for the application time and System.Timestamp for the arrival time. Review the attached end-end flow as follows:

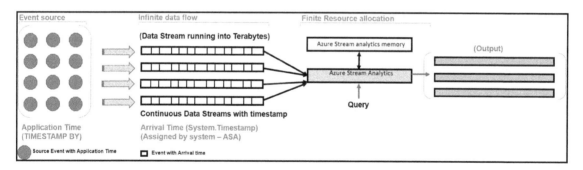

Application and Arrival time

The Application Time with the event payload is set by the user. On the same note the Arrival Time is set by Azure depending on the Azure input source, for example, review the following table. Depending on the Azure resource the Arrival time will be set accordingly:

Azure input resource	Arrival Time
Blob	Blob last modified time (BlobLastModified)
Azure Event Hub	Event Enqueued Time

Azure Stream Analytics is a PaaS service, all the complexities associated with physical infrastructure or configuration is abstracted away. To build a streaming solution without a PaaS based system will involve scores of HW and SW orchestration. In particular when you need to scale up resources to cater surge in demand PaaS based streaming is extremely advantageous.

In the following sections, we will look into key Azure Stream Analytics scaling techniques and close the section with discussions about Embarrassingly parallel jobs and Not embarrassingly parallel as detailed as follows.

Streaming units, partitions, configuring the right type of input, output and query design are the key components that goes into the implementation of a scalable in Azure Stream Analytics.

Streaming Units (**SUs**) is a blend of a resource (CPU, memory, and read and write rates) to execute a given job. Each streaming unit corresponds to roughly 1MB/second of throughput and all queries are executed in memory. Costing is based on the volume of data processed and the number of streaming units required per hour that the job is running.

Costing calculation:

- Volume of streaming data processed
- Compute capacity of the SU

Key factor that will affect the costing of the SU:

- Query complexity, query latency, and the volume of data processed. More complex the query and queries that need multiple steps will increase the cost of the SU. A query can have one or many steps. Each step is a sub-query defined using the **WITH** keyword.
- Depending on the expected performance more streaming units will be required.

- Choosing how many SUs are required for a particular job depends on the partition configuration for the input and the query defined for the job.
- You can select your quota of SUs for a job by using the Azure portal. Each Azure subscription by default has a quota of up to 48 streaming units for all the analytics jobs in a specific region. To increase the SUs for your subscription, log a support ticket through the Microsoft support portal. Do note each SU can process about 1 MB of input.
- The number of SUs that a job can utilize depends on the partition configuration for the input and the query defined for the job. Note a valid value for the stream units must be used. The valid values start at one, three, and six, and then upwards in increments of six.

Partitions

The scaling of a Stream Analytics job takes advantage of partitions in the input or output; partition key enables data to be divided into subsets. A process can consume the subdivided data—such as an Azure Stream Analytics job—and write it into different partitions in parallel, which will increase the throughput significantly. For example, in the following illustration, we are using Event Hubs as scalable event brokers to scale out input:

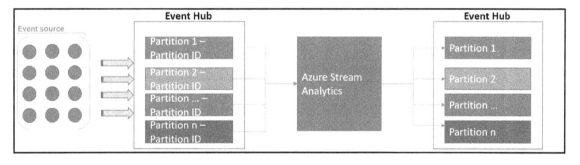

Event Hub ingress and egress with partition

Key advantages of using Event brokers like Event Hub:

- When you use event broker like Event Hub query is partitioned, input events will be processed and aggregated into separate partition groups. To read from Event Hub, ensure that the number of partitions match
- Output events are produced for each partition `group.Partitioning` allows for parallel execution and scale-out. Do note the queries should use **PARTITION BY (Partition Id)** keyword.

In order to build a scalable event broker model like the preceding, we need to have a very clear understanding of the type of input and output that can be used.

In this section, we will review the Input and Output paradigms.

Input source

Following is the full summary of storage type and if it can support parallelization:

Storage Type	Supports Partition Id
• Blob storage • Azure Data Lake Store as Service • Table storage • Event Hub • Cosmos DB • Azure Functions (Preview) • Service Bus Topics • Service Bus Queues	Support Partitioning. Please note if you are using Blob storage • Ensure virtual hierarchy with / • Keep the virtual directory small for performance • Review the full additional tips related to Blob performance `https://docs.microsoft.com/en-us/rest/api/storageservices/naming-and-referencing-containers--blobs--and-metadata` • If you are using Event Hub, you can set the data to have the **PartitionKey** value and it will land on the specific partitions. In case Blob storage dedicated partition folder can be used.
• SQL database (Do note that an SQL server on IaaS is not supported) • Power BI • SQL Data warehouse.	Doesn't support Partitioning

Output source

Following is the full summary of output storage type and support for parallelization:

Storage Type	Parallelizable	Manual/Automatic
Blobs, Tables, ADLS, Service Bus, and Azure Function	Yes	Automatic
CosmosDB and Event Hub	Yes	Manual by specifying **PARTITION BY** field (usually Partition ID). For Event Hub verify the number of portions for inputs and output match to avoid cross-over between partitions.
SQL, SQL DW, and PowerBI	No	Not applicable*

As we reviewed in the previous section, using the right type of Inputs and Output with Partition ID can scale the query parallely. But not all jobs be parallelized. Let's get into the constructs of queries and query parallelization.

Embarrassingly parallel jobs and Not embarrassingly parallel jobs

Embarrassingly parallel jobs are tasks that can be executed independently without any dependency requirement between the tasks. This enables each task to have its process and computing space and in turn, scale parallely to complete the given job faster:

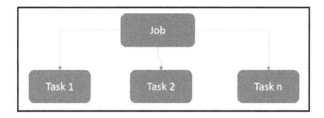

Embarrassingly parallel job

Let's take a simple example, where we are counting, number of a topic from Twitter stream every 10 minutes. The key words to look in this example is the `PARTITION BY PartitionId`. Stream Analytics job takes advantage of partitions in the input or output. `PARTITION BY PartitionId` let's divide the data into subsets based on a partition key. The query will consume and write different partitions in parallel, which increases throughput.

Following is an illustration of tumbling windows for reference purpose:

```
SELECT Count(*) AS Count, Topic
FROM TwitterStream PARTITION BY PartitionId
GROUPBY TumblingWindow(minute,10), Topic, PartitionId
```

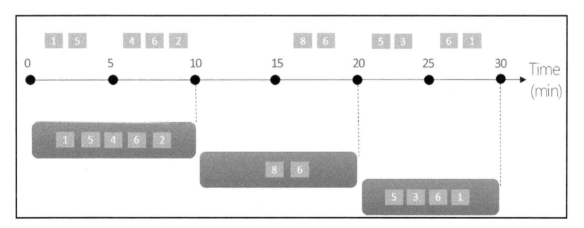

Tumbling windows are continues fixed-sized, non-overlapping and contiguous time intervals

The pictorial view of the how Query will consume data from different partitions from the Event Hub:

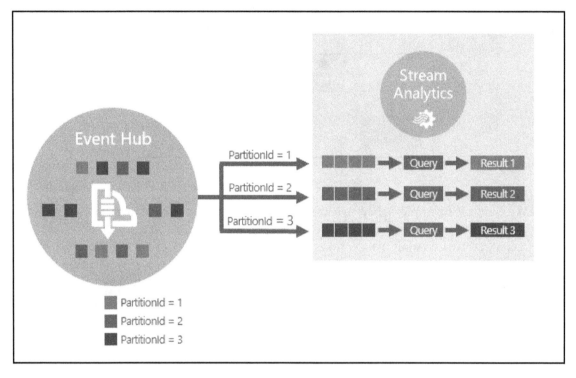

Pictorial view of how the query will get executed in parallel

Summary of the requirement for parallel execution over scaled-out resources:

- The Input source must be partitioned
- The query must-read from the partitioned input source
- The query within the step must have the Partition By keyword

With Not embarrassingly parallel jobs, the tasks get executed have dependency and cannot be executed independently of each other. Due to dependency executing the tasks in parallel becomes challenging. But you can run some of the tasks in parallel:

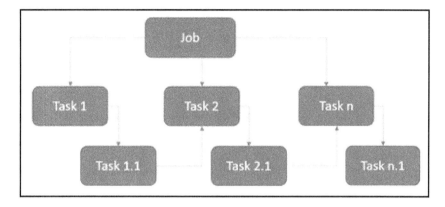

Non-Embarrassingly parallel job

In the following query sample, there are two parts of the query. The first part of the query can be parallelized with the keyword `PartitionID`. The second piece of the query, that's outside the `WITH` construct will not be parallelized. In other words, this is partial parallelization:

```
WITH Step1 AS (
SELECT COUNT(*) AS Count, TollBoothId, PartitionId
FROM Input1 Partition By PartitionId
GROUP BY TumblingWindow(minute, 3), TollBoothId, PartitionId
)
SELECT SUM(Count) AS Count, TollBoothId
FROM Step1
GROUP BY TumblingWindow(minute, 3), TollBoothId
```

Sample deployment of Not embarrassingly parallel deployment using Event Hub and Power BI:

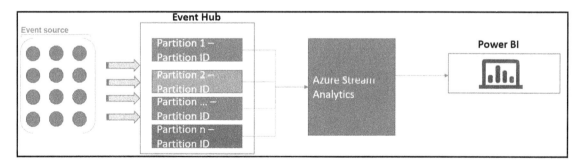

Implementation of Non-Embarrassingly parallel job using Event Hub, Azure Stream Analytics and Power BI

Following are the key points on how to size your scaling units:

- Sizing your **Stream Units (SUs)**:
    - Start your testing with No Partition By with six SU and measure the required performance:
        - If six Streaming unit provides the required performance, leave it as is. You can always try with 3 and 1 Streaming units to gauge the performance
        - Do note single streaming units are not recommended for production workloads
        - Streaming Units depend on a partition configuration for the inputs and on the query defined for the job
    - Streaming units start with 1, 3, 6 and increments of 6 thereafter
    - Non-partitioned steps together can scale up to 6 SUs
    - Each partitioned step can have 6 SUs for each

Sample use case

In this sample, we have a three automated tollbooth and cars pass through every few minutes. The goal is to calculate how many cars have passed through in a given duration.

- No Partition:

```
SELECT COUNT(*) AS Count, TollBoothId
FROM Input1 GROUP BY TumblingWindow(minute, 3), TollBoothId,
PartitionId
```

- Partitioned Query:

```
SELECT COUNT(*) AS Count, TollBoothId
FROM Input1 Partition By PartitionId
GROUP BY TumblingWindow(minute, 3), TollBoothId, PartitionId
```

- Split query with Partition and Non-Partition:

```
WITH Step1 AS (
 SELECT COUNT(*) AS Count, TollBoothId, PartitionId
 FROM Input1 Partition By PartitionId
 GROUP BY TumblingWindow(minute, 3), TollBoothId, PartitionId
 )
 SELECT SUM(Count) AS Count, TollBoothId
 FROM Step1
 GROUP BY TumblingWindow(minute, 3), TollBoothId
```

Summary of the result with the total Streaming Unit:

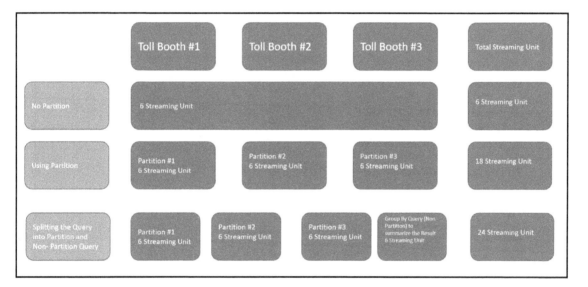

Configuring SU using Azure portal

We will now look into how to scale the SUs for a Stream Analytics job using the Azure portal step by step:

1. Open the job that was previously created in the Azure portal. In the job blade, click the **Scale** option in the **CONFIGURE** section:

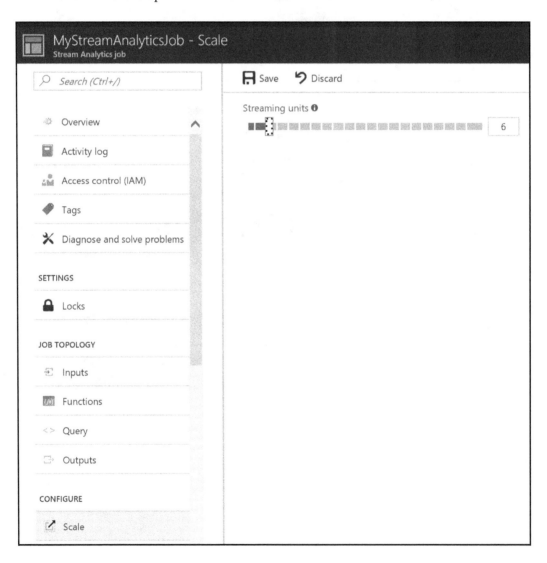

2. Drag the SUs slide to the desired number of units, then click the **Save** button.
3. To monitor how many SUs a job is using, open the job in the Azure portal.
4. In the job blade, click the **Metrics** option in the **Monitoring** section.
5. Under **Available metrics**, select **SU % Utilization**. You can provide a title and subtitle for the metrics chart, change the **Chart type** and **Time range**, and pin the chart to your dashboard. You can also add an alert on the metric as well, so you can receive a notification if the metric exceeds a particular threshold, as follows:

Generally, the **SU % Utilization** number should be at 80% or lower so that there is enough capacity to handle spikes.

6. You can also look at the number of **Input Events** and **Output Events** to measure the throughput of the job as follows:

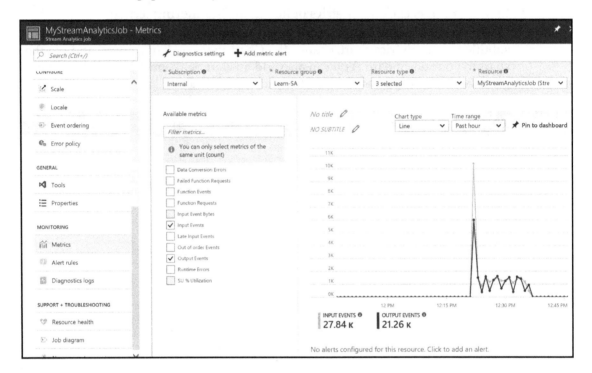

TIP

You can assign one, three, six, or more SUs to a Stream Analytics job. Preceding the six SUs, you must assign SUs in increments of six (for example 12, 18, 24, and so on).

There is a maximum of 200 SUs per subscription, per region. This number can be increased by contacting Microsoft Support. An individual job can have a maximum of 120 SUs, and this limit cannot be increased.

SU utilization can be impacted by stateful processing (windowed aggregates, temporal joins, and temporal analytics functions), which keeps state information using a non-zero Out of order buffer size so that events are reordered, more input partitions, Reference data in joins, and user-defined functions.

Out of order and late-arriving events

The Out of order policy defines a time allowance for events arriving at the Stream Analytics job out of order. It governs how long the Stream Analytics job will buffer events and, within that grace period, corrects the order according to the application timestamp set in the query. While the Out of order events policy is a helpful mechanism by which to manage timing conflicts, it does introduce latency equal to the time allowance duration itself.

Due to connectivity and networking reasons, events generated by source application will arrive out of order. For example in IoT scenario, the connected devices can suffer from intermediate connectivity in which case a set of data will be held on the device that is waiting for a connection to be re-established before the burst is transmitted. Forecasting intermittent device connectivity reliably is a lot more difficult. To address these scenarios, Azure Stream Analytics provides the ability to define a threshold for late arriving events. In summary processing events as they arrive, without reordering, is known as Out of order processing.

Azure Stream Analytics applies temporal transformations when processing incoming events. For handling events that are received out of order, tolerance window can be used to automatically reorder events that arrive within the specified timeframe. If a window is not specified, or if events arrive outside of the window, one of the following actions will be taken: **Drop** or **Adjust**:

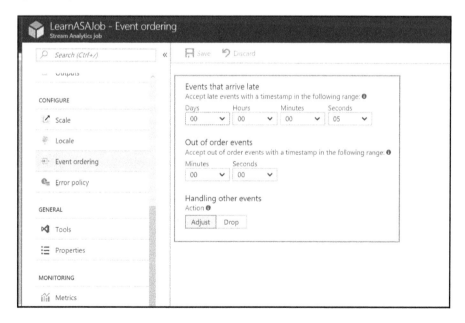

Depending on the scenario, ASA can be configured how to manage events that are received Out of order:

- **Drop**: All events that are received Out of order are dropped (not processed).
- **Adjust**: Timestamps for out of order events are changed to the timestamp of the last correctly ordered event.
- **Tolerance window**: Timestamps of events arriving within the tolerance window will be reordered automatically. Events arriving outside the tolerance window will either be dropped or adjusted based on the out of order policy.

To illustrate, late-arriving events let's take an example of a real-time web analytics scenario, let's say two Event Hubs deployed where one captures impression events, and the other captures click events:

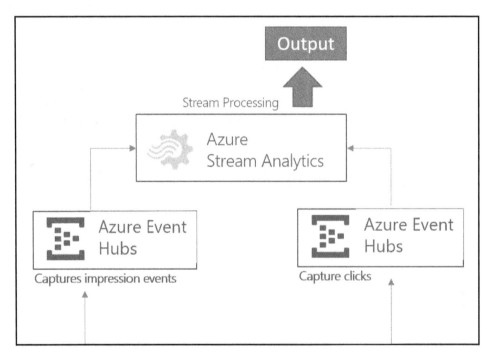

Processing of late arriving events

The stream engine will be required to perform a join between the two incoming streams. One stream representing the impression events would be consumed by the engine, and the second clickstream would also be consumed and joined on one or more key values. To enable this, Azure Stream Analytics allows the join to be defined as valid for a period to allow for late arriving events. For example, in the preceding scenario, it can be configured to be valid for a period of 100 seconds after the impression was served.

Summary

In this chapter, we learnt about how to scale and parallelize Stream Analytics workloads. We explored how to deploy Azure Stream Analytics using ARM templates. Finally, we examined Out of order and late arriving events.

Now that we know how to deploy Azure Stream Analytics and scale it, we will turn to the next chapter to look into other features and functionalities of Azure Stream Analytics.

7
Integration of Microsoft Business Intelligence and Big Data

In this chapter, comparative analysis guidance on Azure Streaming with other Microsoft data platform resources, for example, big data Lambda Architecture integration for real-time data analysis, has been provided and choosing various scenarios for solution architecture designing concepts with Azure HDInsight clusters with Storm and Stream Analytics has been explained. We have portrayed the design and real-world implementation guidelines on near real-time data processing pipelines with a visual dashboard through Azure Stream Analytics and Microsoft Power BI.

This chapter covers the following topics:

- Integration of big data Lambda and Kappa Architecture for real-time data analytics
- Comparative analysis guidance between Azure HDInsight Storm and Stream Analytics
- Step-by-step reference on implementing near real-time data architecture pipeline through designing of a visual dashboard using Stream Analytics and Microsoft Power BI

Nowadays, enterprises don't have to wait for long in a scenario of traditional data processing of bulk-loading massive data and processing through a persistent database through querying and modelling. In today's **Bring Your Own Device (BYOD)** world, you can process data streams in real time with data cleaning, parsing, analyzing, and processing in a single process model. Even with real-time data processing, there is a need for visual dashboards for quick insights from the data. In the Azure data platform, there is a utility of integration of big data Lambda Architecture with implements to Stream Analytics, Azure Event Hub, IoT Hub, Azure Blob storage, Microsoft Power BI, Azure Data Lake, and HDInsight.

There are countless analytics architectural patterns available for data processing and management; Lambda Architecture for big data stands out as a unique and complex design principle, where it addresses the business scenarios demanding the need for data cleaning, parsing, processing, and analyzing huge volumes of data in both batch and interactive modes.

What is Big Data Lambda Architecture?

There are scenarios of fast and slow data processing in terms of hot and cold paths of event streaming respectively in this era of big data and **Internet of Things (IoT)**. In data-oriented software systems, the architecture pattern that has been derived to handle both fast and persistent data paths simultaneously is known as **Lambda Architecture**. It's a powerful data processing pattern utilized for both big data and IoT data processing architectures.

Lambda Architecture gives the benefit of handling massive amounts of petabyte-scale data to be processed both in batch as well as interactive mode.

Concepts of batch processing and stream processing in data analytics

The execution of a job in a series of small processes (batch) is known as **batch processing**, where the input data is divided into a number of chunks with a series of batch jobs. According to Wikipedia, the batch data processing has prevailed from the early nineteenth century for the processing of punch card data used by United States Census Bureau and the first machine-processed data was from batch processing. The concepts of stream processing come with the execution of millions of data streams at an instance with complex event rules.

Streaming frameworks help build near real-time **complex event processing** (**CEP**) platforms, aggregating data from multiple sources such as sensors, web clicks, logs, devices, data warehousing, data marts, telemetry data, and so on, and analyzing and executing through intelligent smart engines such as Azure Stream Analytics.

Specifications for slow/cold path of data - batch data processing

The cold/slow path of data processing refers to the traditional path of data design systems where the massive volume of data is stored at rest in a relational database and persisted. Users, on-demand basis, can query the database and analyze the result in a batch-oriented fashion. This data could be out of date or stored over multiple years persisted on the same database system.

The following traditional batch analytics architecture illustrates this approach:

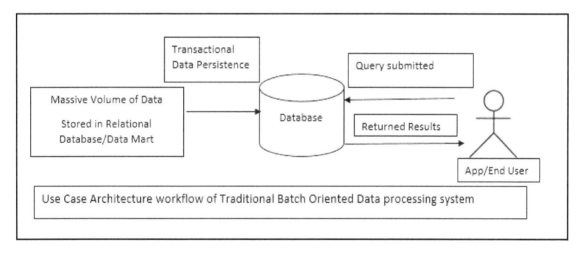

There are several challenges in this traditional batch-oriented architectural model like timeliness of data availability and the possibility of fetching stale data, especially in scenarios of decision support systems. Organisations felt the need of optimizing data processing architectures to process and analyze data at scale and retrieve at the instance, which follows the invention of stream processing systems.

Optionally, many organizations have achieved the capability to support decision-orientated systems by leveraging the ability of fast data processing technologies such as replication of data asynchronously and the transfer of data between transactional operational databases and various analytics repositories. Moreover, the requirement is on a continuous basis and different questions to data analytics require processing the data stream and designing architectures based on the hot (fast) or cold (slow) path of data.

Streaming data technologies refers to the event processing, reactive programming computer paradigm where multiple data computation units can utilize parallel processing explicitly without the intervention of management allocation or data synchronization.

Moving to the streaming-based data solution pattern

Real-time analytics solutions based on event streaming generates several challenges of interactive data at scale. The event-based data processing pattern assists you in moving from point queries against static data. Overall, it's possible to gain insights from data before persisting in the analytics repository.

Enterprises achieve a tremendous advantage of gathering interactive data processing for business challenges along with the capability of archiving the data for long-term storage in stable repositories in order to perform traditional historical data analysis:

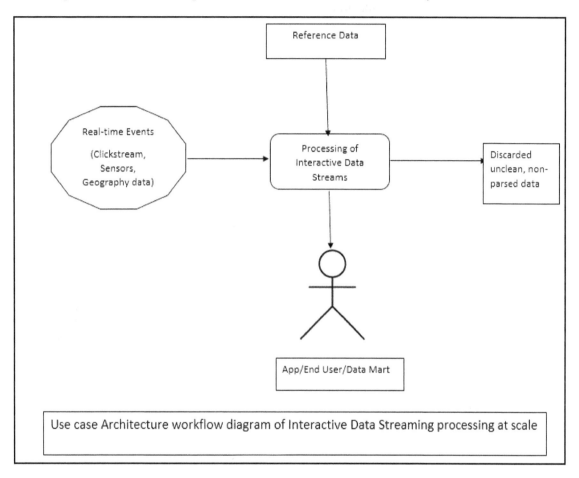

Use case Architecture workflow diagram of Interactive Data Streaming processing at scale

Lambda Architecture typically helps in balancing high availability, fault-tolerance, throughput, latency, the reliability of data at scale with batch processing for historical data analytics, computing data in small jobs as well as processing data at an instance in real-time streams to provide interactive data analytics with visualizations. It consists of three main layers:

- **Batch layer**: This layer precomputes the ingested data at a time and processes in a single job (batch mode), examples being traditional ETL jobs, data warehouses, and data marts. The batch layer is persisted with ingested data on a predefined schedule like once or twice a day or week, month by month, or year by year.
- **Speed layer**: This layer executes complex events as Streams with incremental updates following a complex interactive data model pattern. The Streams update over a few seconds with low latency, high availability, and scalability at an instance.
- **Serving layer**: This computed results of batch and speed layer forms the serving layer that is more an optimized combination of indexing of batch views along with responding queries in an ad hoc manner and implementing interactive visuals.

The advantages of Lambda Architecture are as follows:

- **Predictability of data**, Lambda Architecture in the big data and fast data world helps data talk by analyzing scenarios of when to design by persisted historical data models in traditional data warehouses with precomputed jobs in an ad hoc manner and when to architect complex events designed with interactive stream processing engines to gain insights over a petabyte-scale data
- **Architecture agility**, it is a design pattern that assists you in quickly adopting the changing nature of business predictability in an interactive manner, migrating the path from descriptive analytics to predictive as well as prescriptive analytics

The following image depicts **Big Data Lambda Architecture**:

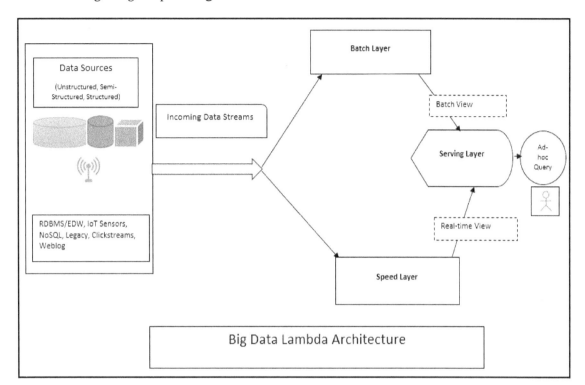

Big Data Lambda Architecture

Evolution of Kappa Architecture and benefits

In 2014, Jay Kreps from LinkedIn first described the concepts of Kappa architecture avoiding the maintenance of a separate code base for batch and real-time data processing. The primary objective is to manage interactive data processing and incremental events updates in a single data stream engine. Kappa Architecture consists of only the speed and serving layer without the batch processing step. The data from the ingestion layer directly move into interactive events processing jobs and the processed data moves into serving layers for near real-time visualization and querying purposes. This architecture follows an event reusable pattern as, for any updates into the stream processing engines, data has to be reprocessed and replied over the previously processed dataset.

The data ingestion layer can be consisted of Publish/Subscribe queue-based messaging systems, such as Apache Kafka, to parse, process, and execute complex events processing in interactive mode, which is generated through Apache Storm or Storm Trident for distributed fault-tolerant, and scalable data patterns. Finally, the serving layer is often designed with either a persisted NoSQL database such as Apache HBase or Cassandra, or a fault-tolerant and distributed Hadoop filesystem such as **Hadoop Distributed File System (HDFS)**, Blob storage, AWS S3, and others.

Similarly, in the Azure-managed data service layer, this architecture could be served by cloud-based Publish/Subscribe queue-oriented near real-time data processing tool. In Azure Data Analytics platform, there are multiple analytics tools. For example, Azure Service Bus Event Hub which is an interactive event ingestion service used as input data stream for Stream Analytics with various job topological output layers to be utilized and designed in serving layers such as Power BI (for interactive analytical data visualization and querying), Azure Data Lake Store (Enterprise scale petabyte-level data store), Azure Blob, Table storage, and SQL database (persistent relational database), Cosmos DB (multi-model of NoSQL data store), Azure Service Bus Queue, Topics, and Azure Event Hub to join further incremental data processing Hubs.

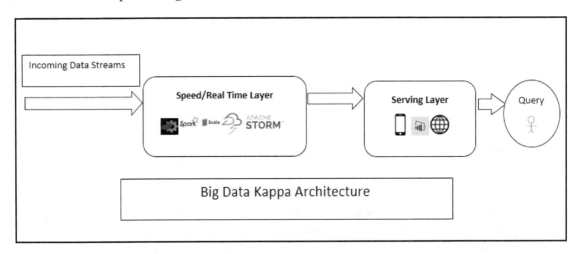

The Lambda and Kappa Architecture model is designed and implemented through big data open source-based technologies such as Apache Storm, Storm Trident, Apache Spark, Spark Streaming, HBase (NoSQL key-value pair data store), Apache Hadoop (HDFS and MapReduce), and Apache Drill; while in the Azure data platform, the interactive or near real-time complex data processing engine could be architectured using open source big data tools on the cloud such as Azure HDInsight (Hadoop), HDInsight Storm, HDInsight Spark, and HDInsight Kafka; managed tools such as Azure Stream Analytics, Azure Service Bus Event Hub, Service Bus Queue, and IoT Hub; persisted storage such as Blob storage; and RDBMS layers such as the Azure SQL database.

Comparison between Azure Stream Analytics and Azure HDInsight Storm

Microsoft announced the availability of a managed real-time data stream engine-Azure Stream Analytics in late 2014, then within a few months, also declared the offering of an interactive open source big data framework—Apache Storm with Azure Hadoop clusters as HDInsight Storm. As an open source tool, Storm with HDInsight has got the capability of integrating with programming languages like Java and Python along with support in Visual Studio IDE using .NET-based APIs for development on Storm applications, Storm HBase, Storm Event Hub, Storm with Document DB/Azure SQL DB reader, and writer sample demos. Both real-time stream processing solutions are offered as managed **Platform as a Service** (**Paas**) models, where users will be charged per unit of clusters and the number of running Storm cluster hours in HDInsight; whereas Stream Analytics charging is based on the provisioned number of Streaming Units and the amount of data processed. The comparison between Azure Stream Analytics and Azure HDInsight Storm is as follows:

Features	Azure HDInsight Storm	Azure Stream Analytics
Scenario	For real-time incremental data processing, Azure HDInsight Storm is observed while the big data architectural patterns like Lambda/Kappa consist of tools more from the Hadoop ecosystem like HDInsight Kafka, integration with Spark, and requires significant custom logic for situations like out of order events, runtime errors, late arrived events, language independence, need to build additional custom data connectors for integration with open source NoSQL data stores such as Mongo DB, Cassandra, AWS Dynamo DB, and Neo4j.	Stream Analytics is a 100% managed service written in .NET, which has a well-defined built-in configuration of reordering events and late arrived erroneous events.
Data Sources	Azure HDInsight Storm has built-in support for reading data connectors such as Service Bus, Event Hub, and Kafka for HDInsight and IoT Hub through custom C#/Java code and output data connectors can be configured with customized logic to serve with HDInsight HBase, Event Hub, SQL DB, Cosmos DB, Blob storage, and Power BI. Connectors can be increased using custom hub/writer applications.	The Azure Streaming job has multiple managed topological input connectors(for example-Event Hub, IoT Hub and Blob Storage) and output connectors such as Azure Blob, SQL DB, Event Hub, Service Bus Queues and Topics, Cosmos DB, Document DB, and Power BI for live visual data streams.
Supported Data Formats	End users can utilize any particular data format by customizing the code (commonly Avro, Parquet, JSON, CSV, TSV, XML, or ORC) to process unstructured, semi-structured, or structured data.	Stream Analytics as a PaaS service has support for only Avro, CSV, and JSON, GZIP and Deflate data formats (as of writing this book) with semi-structured and structured datasets.

Scalability	The HDinsight Storm cluster is configured for scaling by the number and size of worker nodes (for example, the number of Supervisor nodes).	The scalability factor of Streaming Analytics is defined by the number of SUs that are a pool of available computation resources processing the interactive query with the maximum limit of 48 units. SU quota can be even increased by contacting Microsoft Support.
Data processing	Storm with a Trident distributed API provides beneficial functions such as aggregators, joins, grouping, and correlations and possesses guaranteed data processing of at least once delivery. The Trident API uses batch processing and stateful high-level abstractions over the Storm framework.	Azure Stream Analytics provides features for interactive functions with joins, aggregation, and windowing through its rich set of the Query language (named Stream Analytics TSQL Query Language).
Integrity	Storm with HDInsight has support for integration with YARN for data processing using custom code.	Stream Analytics has integration with server architectural components like Azure Functions using output connectors like service queue using Redis Cache, petabyte-scale Enterprise Data Lake Stores like Azure Data Lake. It has managed function service connectors like the JavaScript UDF and Azure Machine Learning as well.
Development	Storm provides comparatively easy, fully customizable, feature-rich APIs with topology consisting of spouts (stream producers) and bolts (stream aggregators), implementing an interactive **directed acyclic graph** (**DAG**) pattern.	Stream Analytics jobs can be created and managed by an Azure portal, Visual Studio tools for ASA, or through **Azure Resource Manager** (**ARM**) deployment scripts.

Fault Tolerance	Apache Storm has a built-in capability of fault tolerance where its master (Nimbus) and supervisor nodes are designed to be fail-fast (self-destructing methods for any disaster handling).	Stream Analytics processes job reliability avoiding failures and service interruptions through the Azure Paired Region model, where event processing jobs are updated in isolated batches on another paired regional data center utilizing significant time delay for incremental updates and identifying faults to remediate.
Debugging and Monitoring	Storm UI has support for live monitoring of tuples and bolts, and topology structures with a detailed job execution status report. Debugging and monitoring for Storm HDI clusters can also be customized through code using the REST API.	Near real-time live monitoring, support is provided by the Azure portal, Visual Studio ASA tools, and REST API. Stream Analytics also supports Azure alerts for metrics (for example, %SU utilization, runtime errors, out of order events, and functional errors) and activity logs basis. Diagnostics logs can even be configured for streaming jobs in the Azure portal and through the REST API.

Designing data processing pipeline of an interactive visual dashboard through Stream Analytics and Power BI

The serving layer in big data Lambda/Kappa Architecture provides real-time transient views along with an ad hoc querying functionality. In designing the complex data architecture pipeline, the benefits of processed results through a near real-time analytics dashboard is inevitable. Azure Stream Analytics a managed complex event processing interactive data engine. As a built-in output connector, it offers the facility of building live interactive intelligent BI charts and graphics using Microsoft's cloud-based Business Intelligent tool called Power BI.

Prerequisites of building an interactive visual live dashboard in Power BI with Stream Analytics:

The following resources are required for implementing live visuals with PowerBI integrated as output for Stream Analytics job.

- Azure subscription
- Power BI Office365 account (the account email ID should be the same for both Azure and Power BI). It can be a work or school account

Integrating Power BI as an output job connector for Stream Analytics

To start with connecting the Power BI portal as an output of an existing Stream Analytics job, follow the given steps:

1. First, select **Outputs** in the Azure portal under **JOB TOPOLOGY**:

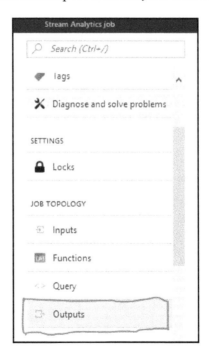

2. After clicking on **Outputs**, click on **+Add** in the top left corner of the job window, as shown in the following screenshot:

3. After selecting **+Add**, you will be prompted to enter the **New output** connectors of the job. Provide details such as job Output name/alias; under **Sink**, choose **Power BI** from the drop-down menu.

4. On choosing **Power BI** as the streaming job output Sink, it will automatically prompt you to authorize the Power BI work/personal account with Azure. Additionally, you may create a new Power BI account by clicking on **Signup**. By authorizing, you are granting access to the Stream Analytics output permanently in the Power BI dashboard. You can also revoke the access by changing the password of the Power BI account or deleting the output/job.

5. Post the successful authorization of the Power BI account with Azure, there will be options to select **Group Workspace**, which is the Power BI tenant workspace where you may create the particular dataset to configure processed Stream Analytics events. Furthermore, you also need to define the **Table Name** as data output. Lastly, click on the **Create** button to integrate the Power BI data connector for real-time data visuals:

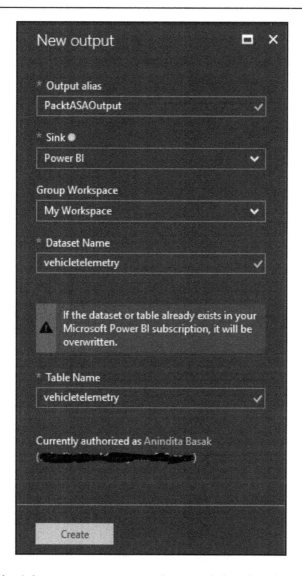

If you don't have any custom workspace defined in the Power BI tenant, the default workspace is **My Workspace**. If you define a dataset and table name that already exists in another Stream Analytics job/output, it will be overwritten. It is also recommended that you just define the dataset and table name under the specific tenant workspace in the job portal and not explicitly create them in Power BI tenants as Stream Analytics automatically creates them once the job starts and output events start to push into the Power BI dashboard.

6. On starting the Streaming job with output events, the Power BI dataset would appear under the dataset tab following workspace. The dataset can contain maximum 200,000 rows and supports real-time streaming events and historical BI report visuals as well:

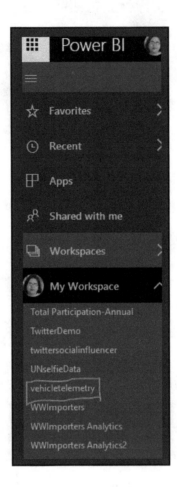

7. Further Power BI dashboard and reports can be implemented using the streaming dataset. Alternatively, you may also create tiles in custom dashboards by selecting **CUSTOM STREAMING DATA** under **REAL-TIME DATA**, as shown in the following screenshot:

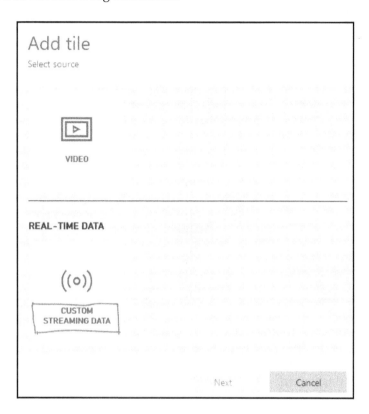

8. By selecting **Next**, the streaming dataset should be selected and then the visual type, respective fields, Axis, or legends, can be defined:

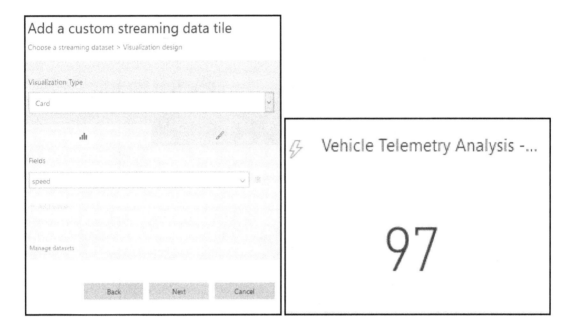

9. Thus, a complete interactive near real-time Power BI visual dashboard can be implemented with analyzed streamed data from Stream Analytics, as shown in the following screenshot, from the real-world Connected Car-Vehicle Telemetry analytics dashboard:

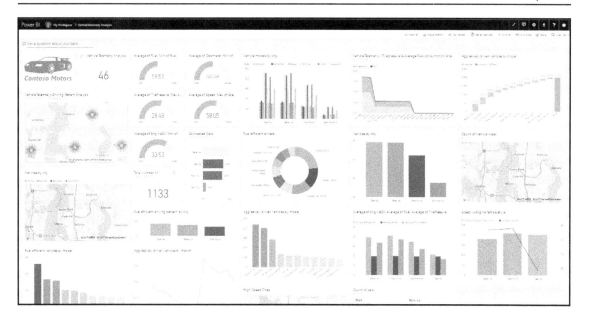

Summary

In this chapter, you have learned about big data architectural patterns such as Lambda and Kappa for historical and interactive complex stream processing along with in-depth analysis of batch processing and the speed and serving layer for ad hoc querying. In the real world, the big and fast data processing pipeline follows mostly Lambda or Kappa design patterns from events ingestion to processing and finally implementing near real-time intelligent visual dashboards. We have provided step-by-step guidance of developing a real-time visual dashboard using Microsoft Power BI with processed data from Azure Stream Analytics as the output data connector.

In the next chapter, we will be concentrating on designing and managing Stream Analytics jobs using reference data and utilizing petabyte-scale enterprise data store with Azure Data Lake Store and a globally distributed NoSQL database from Microsoft Azure Cosmos DB—and the next generation server-less cloud architectures with Azure Functions.

8
Designing and Managing Stream Analytics Jobs

In an Enterprise Data Lake scenario, there is a requirement for integrating complex event and streaming architectures with Azure data services resources, such as petabyte scale, big data-Hadoop equivalent file system repositories (Azure Data Lake Store), and a NoSQL multi-modeled, globally-scaled databases such as Azure Cosmos DB, and utilizing serverless configuration streams in a response to events (Azure Functions).

This chapter focuses on:

- Designing and managing data sources from Azure reference events (Blob storage)
- Enhancing interactive events with Azure Stream Analytics data sinks such as Azure Data Lake and Azure Cosmos DB
- How to elevate serverless architecture configuration using Azure Functions

In a complex event processing scenarios, a fully managed event execution engine like Azure Stream Analytics offers very low latency along with support for consistent, historical, or long-term data, and static data such as an event input stream. Similarly, Azure Stream Analytics is compatible with the globally-distributed, multi-model, NoSQL-based, JSON data-oriented, database Azure Cosmos DB, which supplies a partitioned collection for the partitioning output data, for optimized performance. The output data sink connector of Stream Analytics also provides integration with the serverless architecture resources on Azure, such as function apps by connecting with Azure Service Bus events or through Azure Cosmos DB binding triggers.

Reference data streams with Azure Stream Analytics

Reference data can be static or finite datasets which are slowly modifying, executed to perform a lookup, or joining/correlating input data streams of Azure Stream Analytics. Reference data streams supported by Azure Blob storage have a limit of 100 MB per Blob, but each Stream Analytics job can execute multiple Blobs with appropriate path patterns simultaneously. Reference data Blobs support a collection of file streams by partitioning through the same **date/time** identifiers as the name of the Blob. Each Blob is concatenated at the end of the Blob collection sequence, by specifying a date/time identifier greater than the last modified Blob in the sequence.

Configuration of Reference data for Azure Stream Analytics jobs

In order to configure the reference data stream for an Azure Stream Analytics job, the static dataset needs to be uploaded first as reference data to the Azure Block Blob storage, using Azure SDK/CLI/PowerShell/Azure Portal/Azure Storage Explorer.

The following configuration properties must be carried out for integrating the Azure Blob storage as reference data:

- **Input alias**: The ASA job reference input name used to specify the reference data
- **Source Type**: Reference data needs to be specified for the job. There are two types of data input sources, **data stream** and **reference data**
- **Storage Account Name**: The Azure Blob storage account name must be specified, either the same Azure subscription or a different subscription
- **Storage Account Key**: The account secret key associated with the storage account configured as the reference stream

- **Container Name**: Logical groups of Blobs where the reference streams need to be stored
- **Path pattern**: The location path of the block Blob files defined within the specified container. The path provides the file reference paths supplied with backslashes such as (`iotdelivery/{date}/{time}/devicerules.json`)
- **Date Format**: While the **Date** is used within the path pattern of the reference data Blobs, the formatting of the date can be specified from the available drop-down options (for example, MM/DD/YYYY, DD-MM-YYYY, YYYY/DD/MM, and so on)
- **Time Format**: The time format can also be specified using the available formats from the drop-down menu (HH, HH-mm, HH/mm)
- **Encoding**: The default encoding format for the reference data stream of Stream Analytics jobs is UTF-8

Integrating a reference data stream as job topology input for an Azure Stream Analytics job

For integrating a reference data stream as an input event for a Stream Analytics job we must perform the following:

1. First, select **Inputs** under the **JOB TOPOLOGY** section and click on the **Add icon**
   .

2. The **New Input** job topology prompt will appear for have configured the Reference data (Blob storage) stream.

3. Providing the job **Input alias** name. The **Source Type** should be specified as **Reference data**. The Blob storage account name, account key, container name, path pattern, date/time format, and so on need to be provided manually.

4. If the Blob storage account details are imported from a current Azure subscription, then the storage account name can be selected from the available drop-down menu and its account secret key and container name should be populated:

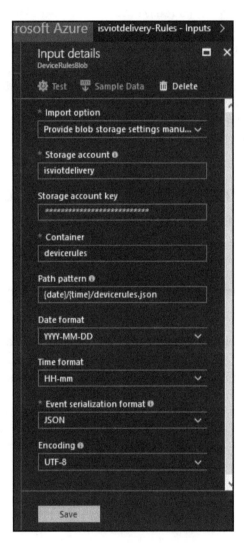

If your Azure Stream Analytics job and reference stream Blob storage are located in different regions, then data transfer charges will be applicable.

Stream Analytics query configuration for Reference Data join

The Reference data stream from the Azure Blob storage needs a JOIN clause with the Event Hub/IoT Hub data input stream. For example, in this predictive analytics demo, the Reference data stream (DeviceRulesBlob) is correlated with an IoT Hub input stream (IotTelemetryStream), with weather sensor data schemas such as humidity, temperature, and so on.

The example that follows is a Stream Analytics IoT Sensor Data Analytics job query with reference stream JOIN IoT Hub data input events:

```
WITH AlarmsData AS
(
SELECT
Stream.IoTHub.ConnectionDeviceId AS DeviceId,
'Temperature' as ReadingType,
Stream.Temperature as Reading,
Ref.Temperature as Threshold,
Ref.TemperatureRuleOutput as RuleOutput,
Stream.EventEnqueuedUtcTime AS [Time]
FROM IoTTelemetryStream Stream
JOIN DeviceRulesBlob Ref ON Stream.IoTHub.ConnectionDeviceId = Ref.DeviceID
WHERE
Ref.Temperature IS NOT null AND Stream.Temperature > Ref.Temperature
UNION ALL
SELECT
Stream.IoTHub.ConnectionDeviceId AS DeviceId,
'Humidity' as ReadingType,
Stream.Humidity as Reading,
Ref.Humidity as Threshold,
Ref.HumidityRuleOutput as RuleOutput,
Stream.EventEnqueuedUtcTime AS [Time]
FROM IoTTelemetryStream Stream
JOIN DeviceRulesBlob Ref ON Stream.IoTHub.ConnectionDeviceId = Ref.DeviceID
WHERE
Ref.Humidity IS NOT null AND Stream.Humidity > Ref.Humidity
)
SELECT *
INTO DeviceRulesMonitoring
FROM AlarmsData
```

Refresh schedule of a reference data stream

- The overwriting steps of reference data streams using Azure Blobs do not refresh new Blobs. It's recommended to create a new block Blob in an Azure storage account used as a reference stream, storing new Blob data in a separate container with specified path patterns, identified by the date/time parameter modified to a greater value than the last Blob provided in the collection.

- The reference data stream updates or modifies, this is not based on the Blob's **last modified time**, but the date/time identifier provided in the Reference data path pattern.

- Since the Reference data stream input for an Azure Stream Analytics job is static or slow changing in nature, the refresh option is enabled by defining `{date}/{time}` configuration parameters (for example, DD-MM-YYYY, or MM/DD/YYYY, YYYY-DD-MM / HH-mm, and so on) in the job input settings substitution token values.

- If the path pattern of a reference data input of a Stream Analytics job is defined as `{date}/{time}/devicerules.json` with the `{Time}` format parameterized in HH-mm style, and the job is started then the job will refreshed with a new, updated block Blob file (for example, `2017-10-03/15:00/devicerules1.json` by 3rd October, 2017 at 3 PM UTC.

Configuration of output data sinks for Azure Stream Analytics with Azure Data Lake Store

The Azure Data Lake Store is an Enterprise level petabyte scale, big data store available in the Microsoft Cloud with similar interfaces as **Hadoop file system** (**HDFS**) and integrates well with Hadoop ecosystems like the Spark, Storm, Sqoop, YARN, or MapReduce. The Azure Data Lake Store follows a massive, parallel processing POSIX file system structure, and is capable of storing a lot of unstructured/semi-structured data. In **complex event processing** (**CEP**) scenarios, Azure Data Lake Store provides the flexibility of storing big data analytics workloads from batch or event processing, IoT machine learning streams, and so on. For data operation, Data Lake Store provides enterprise graded authentication support integration with the Azure active directory identity mode, authorization is designed with POSIX **access control lists** (**ACL**) maintaining WebHDFS-managing the REST API as a server-side API with hierarchical file system volumes.

Configuring Azure Data Lake Store as an output data sink of Stream Analytics

Azure Data Lake store can now be integrated as an output data sink for Stream Analytics. Before, the enterprise Data Lake Store needed to be provisioned either from Azure portal/CLI/PowerShell. It offers the creation of an ADLS accounts using a developer SDK available in Java, .NET, Python/Node.js, and supports Visual Studio 2017/2015 IDE as well.

- Azure Data Lake Store recommends encryption of data at rest, utilizing server managed keys or client managed keys used through the Azure Key Vault.
- **OAuth 2.0** is the protocol used by Azure Data Lake Store for data authorization protocol, along with the support of role-based access control by Azure Active Directory identities.
- At the time of provisioning the Data Lake Store, the encryption option is provided either to enable managing keys by Data Lake Store or using them from a Key Vault in case of enabling the encryption:

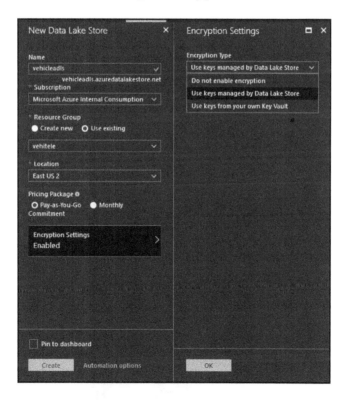

Configuring Azure Data Lake Store as an output sink of Stream Analytics jobs

In order to configure the Azure Data Lake Store as an output sink of a Stream Analytics job, the Data Lake Store account credentials need to be imported either from the same subscription or entered manually:

1. From the **JOB TOPOLOGY** settings of a Stream Analytics job, select **Outputs** and enter the **Data Lake Store** output account alias name.

2. Define the data **Sink** type as `Azure Data Lake Store` for capturing unstructured/semi-structured/quasi-structured data petabyte volumes, with speed targeted to be utilized in operational and exploratory big data analytics.

3. You will be prompted to authorize the Data Lake Store connection with the available provisioned Data Lake Store accounts in your Azure subscription. If you don't have any Azure Data Lake Store account available in your subscription, you can sign up by following this step:

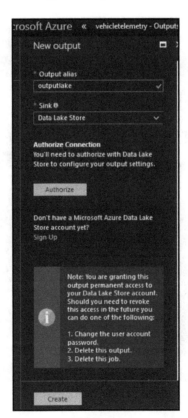

4. Upon authorizing, the **Import** option will appear in the **New output** configuration settings. You can select Data Lake Store either from your subscription, or you can provide Data Lake Store details manually.

5. On specifying the correct Azure subscription and Data Lake account name you need to define the **Path prefix pattern,** which provides the file path demonstrating the location of your output data files within your Azure Data Lake Store account in the format of **cluster/folder/{date}/{time}** as an example. In this Vehicle Predictive Analytics demo, the **Path prefix pattern** is `VehicleTelemetry/logs/{date}/{time}`. Within this file path, multiple instances can be provided using `{date}` and `{time}` as identifiers.

6. Defining path patterns with `{date}` and `{time}` identifiers, the date and time format can also be chosen from the available formatting options (such as YYYY/MM/DD or MM-DD-YYYY, HH-mm for time format options, and so on).

7. Next, the available event serialization patterns for Data Lake events such as JSON, CSV, or Avro format, with encoding set to UTF-8, should be formatted either as Line Separated or as an Array types. JSON object events will be separated by newlines for **Line Separated** mode and should be constructed as an **Array** type data event structure if the Array type format is used for processing output events in an Azure Data Lake Store account.

8. Finally, the **Create** button should be clicked in order to integrate the Azure Data Lake store as an output connector of Stream Analytics to store big data, volume level, and hyperscale massive parallel processed data from Stream Analytics:

Integration of Azure Data Lake Store as output connector of Stream Analytics job:

Integration of Azure Data Lake Store as output connector of Stream Analytics job

The Solution Architecture workflow of Vehicle Telemetry Analytics using Azure Data Lake Store is as follows:

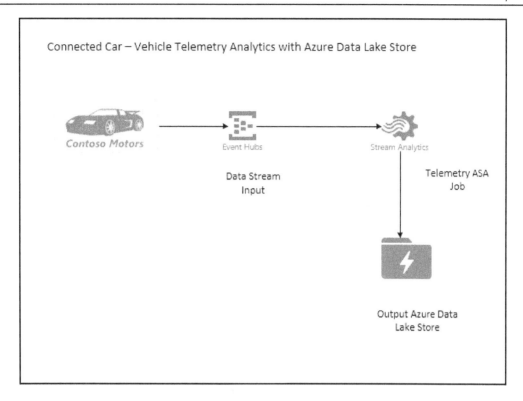

Connected Car – Vehicle Telemetry Analytics with Azure Data Lake Store

9. The processed output in Azure Data Lake Store can be observed from the **Data Explorer** menu under **Data Lake Store** settings. Select the appropriate folder configured in the output settings with the (**Directory/Folder/{Year}/{Date}/{Time}**) path pattern as defined in the output sink settings of the Stream Analytics job:

Configuring Azure Cosmos DB as an output data sink for Azure Stream Analytics

In the NoSQL world, Azure Cosmos DB is the first to provide support of document-orientated, graph-based, key-value pairs and column-family based databases on a globally-distributed, horizontally-scaled, backed, highly-available databases. Azure Cosmos DB provides elastic scale-out capability across all available Azure geographic regions offering guaranteed low latency, replication of data globally, multi-model compute, and storage, including five consistency models:

1. In order to configure **Azure Azure Cosmos DB** as an output sink for Stream Analytics, we need to provide the Azure Cosmos DB account first with the appropriate **collection ID** and **database** list.

2. From the Azure portal, Click on **New** and under **Databases**, select **Azure Cosmos DB** to start provisioning the account:

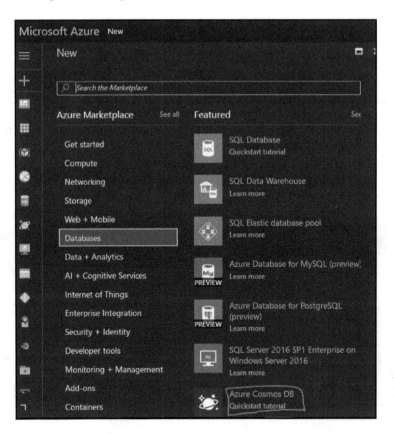

3. Next, provide the **Cosmos Db Account Id (Name)**, **API type (SQL as DocumentDb**, **MongoDB**, **Graph as Gremin API**, **or Table as key-value paired API)**, subscription details, and the resource manager credentials. Also, there's an option to select the checkbox to enable automated pairing of Cosmos DB Accounts with multiple other Azure regions by clicking on the **enable geo-redundancy** checkbox, and finally hitting the **Create** button to start the provisioning Azure Cosmos DB:

4. While it's in the deploying phase, you may track the provisioning status on the Azure portal homepage:

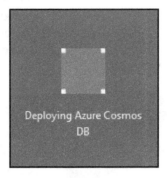

5. Now, just after the provisioned phase, you will need to provide the Collection IDs and database details associated with the Azure Cosmos DB using .NET/ Java/.NET core/Xamarin/Node.js/Python, and so on. Select **.NET** as a type of document and specify collection ID and database name in order to integrate an output sink of a Stream Analytics job:

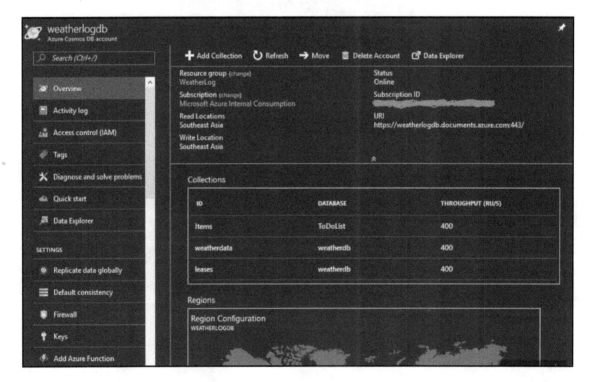

If you don't create a custom document Collection ID and database for your Azure Cosmos DB account, there's always a default collection ID named **Items** and database called **ToDoList**.

Features of Azure Cosmos DB for configuring output sinks of Azure Stream Analytics

The Azure Cosmos DB provides a guaranteed SLA with throughput, low latency, and high availability suitable for mission-critical applications. It supports multi-model, SQL, and open source APIs as data models for APIs:

- The Azure Cosmos DB offers multi-homing APIs which help to provide the lowest latency to customers by providing responses from the nearest Azure data center with no additional application level configuration changes. Multiple read-regions can be specified as well with respect to write-region.
- Cosmos DB has the feature of always-on **high availability** with **99.99 %** guaranteed SLA benefits, which are inevitable for designing analysis and storage integration layers for complex event processing scenarios.
- There are five consistency models available with Azure Cosmos DB, but one database in the cloud covering both SQL-like consistency with all the aspects of NoSQL like eventual consistency and graph-based networking data layers with a key-value pair models.
- Completely schema-agnostic, the Azure Azure Cosmos DB offers dynamic indexes to all data ingested.

Configuring Azure Cosmos DB integrated with Azure Stream Analytics as an output sink

To add Azure Cosmos DB as an output data connector of Azure Stream Analytics jobs, follow the given steps:

1. You need to select the output sink type as **Azure Cosmos DB** under the **Outputs** section of **JOB TOPOLOGY** and confirm that the Azure Cosmos DB account is already provisioned with the appropriate Collection ID and database:

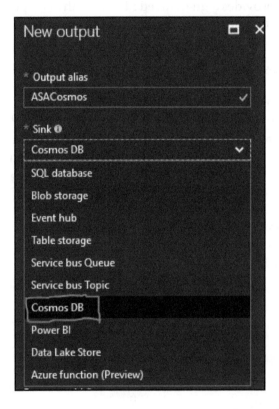

2. Next, select the Azure Cosmos DB account ID and the database name, and provide the proper collection ID of the document database and document ID since for this weather telemetry demo. I've used a Document DB (SQL)-type API of the Cosmos DB account, configured as an output of a Stream Analytics job. Finally, click **Create** to finish the configuration.

3. Once the Stream Analytics job is started, you can see the weather telemetry sensor data indexes with the ID and Cosmos DB partition key defined as **AirportID** for this weather telemetry analytics demo in the Cosmos DB collections under the **Data Explorer** section of the Azure portal:

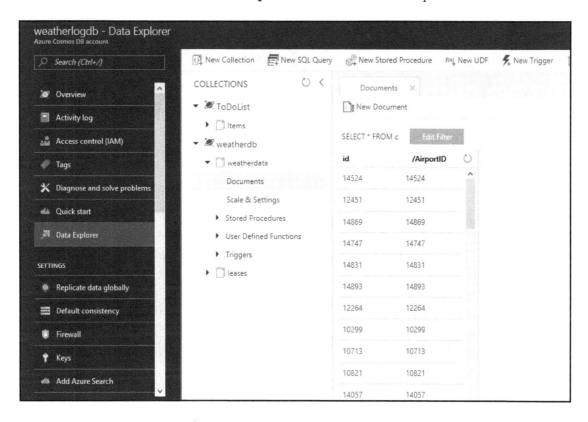

4. From the **Query Explorer** under **Collections**, choose the query, selecting the weather sensor data telemetry database and collections, and execute the query. The results will be available in JSON format with a partition keys such as AirportID, WindSpeed, WindDirection, DewPoint, and so on:

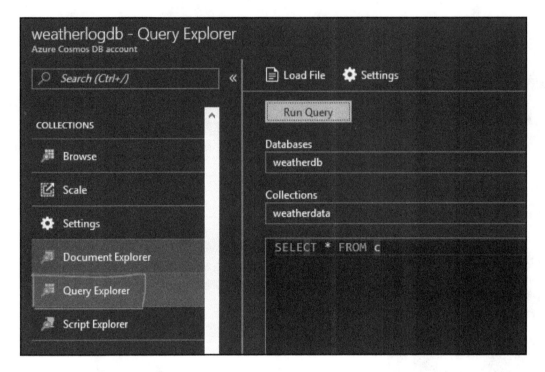

The results of the Cosmos DB document API of weather telemetry analytics output in the JSON format, processed through Azure Stream Analytics is as follows:

osoft Azure

Home > weatherlogdb - Query Explorer > Results

Results
SELECT * FROM c

→ Next page

```
{
    "AirportID": "14524",
    "Year": "2013",
    "Month": "07",
    "Day": "31",
    "Time": "2334",
    "TimeZone": "-5",
    "SkyCondition": "SCT003 OVC070",
    "Visibility": "2.50",
    "WeatherType": "BR",
    "DryBlubFarenheit": "72",
    "DryBulbCelsius": "22.0",
    "WetBulbFarenheit": "71",
    "WetBulbCelsius": "21.4",
    "DewPointFarenheit": "70",
    "DewPointCelsius": "21.0",
    "RelativeHumidity": "93",
    "WindSpeed": "7",
    "WindDirection": "130",
    "ValueForWindCharacter": "",
    "StationPressure": "29.85",
    "PressureTendency": "",
    "PressureChange": "",
    "SeaLevelPressure": "M",
```

Stream Analytics job output to Azure Function Apps as Serverless Architecture

In Serverless computing, without designing complex nodes and modules, there's a possibility to create scalable, loosely-coupled pieces of logic to execute on demand without provisioning or managing the detailed infrastructure in the cloud. The Azure Functions provide such benefits by applying event-driven computing at scale based on-triggers, or HTTP event requests/webhooks. Azure Function apps provide a fully-managed abstraction of servers and infrastructure and operating, without the hassle of managing system administration and event-driven, API-oriented trigger systems in near-time. This allows developers to focus on apps and flexible scaling while paying for only the resources running over seconds to milliseconds.

Provisioning steps to an Azure Function

In order to get started with serverless computing using an Azure Function, first, you need to provision the Function app either from Azure portal, CLI, or PowerShell/.NET SDK:

1. From the Azure Portal, Under **New** | **Azure Marketplace**, select the **Function App** from the **Compute** section:

2. Provide the **name** of the function and select the **resource group**. The **hosting plan** can be chosen as the **Consumption plan** as part of a pay-as-you-go pricing, which and allows billing only for resources executed from a few seconds to milliseconds, and based on new resources allocation, in scaling on-demand capacity. A default storage account is also associated with provisioning of a **Function App**. For monitoring of .NET app issues, services like **Application Insights** can be turned **On** optionally as well for Azure functions:

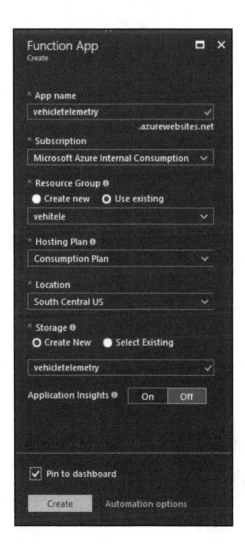

3. On clicking the **Create** button, it will validate the Function app template and provision default a Function app where triggers, timers, or data processing can be set using C#, Java, JavaScript, or F#:

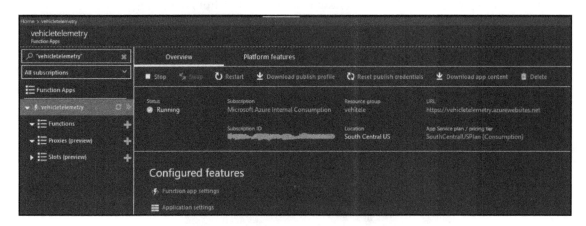

4. Click on the + icon beside **Functions** and choose the scenario: **Timer** or **Data processing.** Language can be selected as C# and hit on **Create** this function from **quickstart template:**

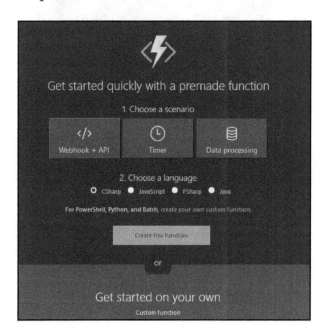

Configuring an Azure function as a serverless architecture model integrated with Stream Analytics job output

An Azure function as a serverless computing model can be triggered based on events from an Azure Stream Analytics job and finally, can be processed through input or output binding Azure Cosmos DB. For example, in this following solution architecture, a connected car-vehicle telemetry predictive health analytics scenario, the Azure Cosmos DB output binding is integrated with an Azure Function triggered from the Event Hub, configured as an output sink of the vehicle telemetry Stream Analytics job:

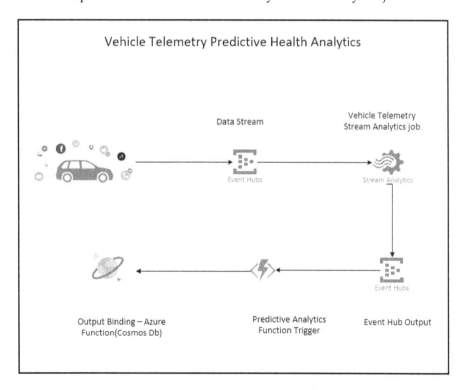

The Solution Architecture of Connected Car-Vehicle Telemetry Predictive Health Analytics with an Azure function triggered by Azure Cosmos DB output binding

For configuring an Azure function as an **event-based trigger** model for Stream Analytics job output, implement the following steps:

1. In this demo of vehicle telemetry analytics, use the ConnectedCar Stream Analytics job, where the output events are passed through another Service Bus Event Hub configured with the car telemetry partition key (`VehicleIndexNo`):

2. Next, the complex analyzed events can be triggered through the Azure Function app. From the **Function** app, optionally using the **custom template function**, a custom function trigger can be chosen, for example, in this vehicle telemetry connected car analytics demo, an **EventHubTrigger - C# function** is select to execute and notify a **CollectionId** through Azure Azure Cosmos DB whenever a new processed vehicle health predictive schema changes based on a webhook event index, Vehicle Index no:

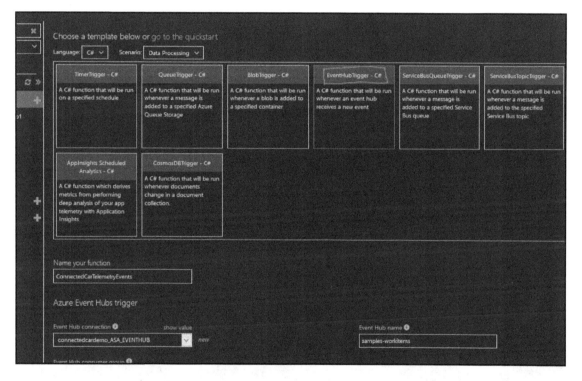

3. While choosing the **EventHubTrigger C#** function, the details of the Service Bus Event Hub configurations can be provided such as **Function name**, **Event Hub connection**, **Event Hub name**, and so on.

4. In the **Functions** pane, select the **EventHubTrigger** function and in the run.csx file, provide the following serverless event triggers to send a notification for a new stream entry in the VehicleEventOut Event Hub:

```
using System;
public static void Run(string ConnectedCarTelemetry, TraceWriter
log)
{
log.Info($"New Telemetry Event Triggered for Connected Car:
{ConnectedCarTelemetry}");
}
```

The output of the preceding code is:

5. Next, configure the output event of an Azure function integrated with the multi-model, globally distributed Azure Cosmos DB data collection. From the **Integrate** menu, select **+New Output** and choose **Azure Azure Cosmos DB** as the output event store. Finally, click on **Select** to start associating the **Azure Cosmos DB** account as an output event trigger for an Azure Function:

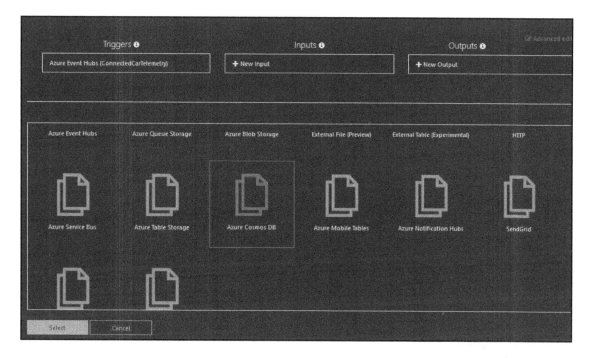

6. In the subsequent step, the Azure Cosmos DB account details, like **Document parameter name, Azure Cosmos DB database name, Collection id, Azure Cosmos DB account connection string, partition key** (optional) are required. To create the respective document data Collection ID and database, if they don't exist, check the following checkbox the database name textbox (if true, creates the document database and collection):

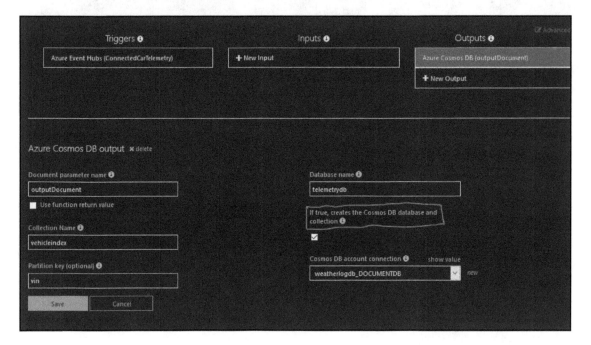

7. Finally, the output data trigger can be observed from the data explorer window of the respective Azure Cosmos DB in the **Documents** section of the **telemetrydb** database for the **vehicleindex** collection:

 Optionally, the output events through the Event Hub from the Connected Car-Vehicle Telemetry Predictive Analytics Stream Analytics job can be captured to an Azure Event Grid--Serverless event computing model by topic, and then be published into the final output of a VehicleTelemetry-Azure function.

At the time of writing, the Azure Event Grid and Azure Function connector for Stream Analytics is in the preview, stage suitable for only dev or test environments. It is not recommended for the production environments yet.

Summary

In this chapter, you gained a well-versed, in-depth learning of high-level design with real-world data streaming architecture components, and understanding of the usage of reference data streams and the output data sink layers using hyperscale big data storage in Azure, also known as the Azure Data Lake Store. We also learned about the globally-distributed, multi-model, low latency, elastic, scale-out capabilities of managing data at a global scale. We have also learned how to architect serverless event processing using the Azure functions with the Azure Cosmos DB output triggers.

In the next chapter, we will learn how to design the integration of intelligence in Azure Streaming, utilizing Azure Machine Learning, Javascript user-defined functions with complex streams, and finally will implement interactive data stream pipeline application building concepts using the Azure .NET management SDK.

9

Optimizing Intelligence in Azure Streaming

In modern Cloud Data Analytics Architecture, there is a need for the optimization of platform solution designs with the highest level of intelligence through smart machine learning algorithms, building predictive models using advanced DevOps functions with conceptualizing, wrangling, and modelling, and finally implementation of an advanced real-time data streaming pipeline. In this chapter, you will learn how to architect an optimized and intelligent advanced streaming data platform with the Azure Data Analytics pipeline by leveraging smart algorithms integrated with Stream Analytics:

- Utilizing JavaScript **user-defined function (UDF)** with an Azure Streaming query
- Integrating intelligent Azure machine learning algorithms with Stream Analytics functions
- Developing a data streaming application by implementing a Stream Analytics job code structure with .NET management SDK

Real-time streaming data has the benefits of the generation of complex event processing dynamic data over a second or millisecond interval in a micro-batch-oriented fashion from various data sources like IoT sensors, telemetry sources, social media feeds and live streams, weblog clickstreams, and so on. Applying intelligent Azure ML functions and JavaScript UDF on streaming jobs to process the queries in a live fashion is a result of retrieving the analyzed data streams with smart function algorithms.

Integration of JavaScript user-defined functions using Azure Stream Analytics

JavaScript user-defined functions with the enhanced support of String, Math, Array, Date, regular expressions, Integer to Float conversion, and hex to decimal/binary/integer functions are supported with Azure Stream Analytics to apply query transformation, on streaming data. These functions provide generic stateless computation values applied to input data streams or reference data streams of Stream Analytics without plugging into any data source.

The JavaScript UDF for Stream Analytics jobs are advantageous in the following domains:

- Data Streams with string manipulation with JavaScript regular expression functions like `Regexp`, along with String methods like extract (`Regexp_extract`), replace (`Regexp_replace`), match (`Regexp_match`), and split (`Regexp_split`)
- Data events conversion, for example, Hex to Integer, decimal to binary, and data encoding/decoding
- Mathematical and statistical function computations on complex events
- Event correlation, lookups, aggregation, data input streams joining operations. and much more

Adding JavaScript UDF with a Stream Analytics job

The JavaScript functions can be integrated with Stream Analytics jobs and called from an ASA SQL query as a function of the Azure portal:

1. From the Azure portal in your **Stream Analytics job**, under **JOB TOPOLOGY**, choose **Functions**:

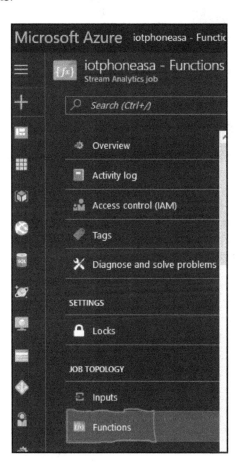

2. Click on the **+Add** icon to assimilate JavaScript function with the ASA job:

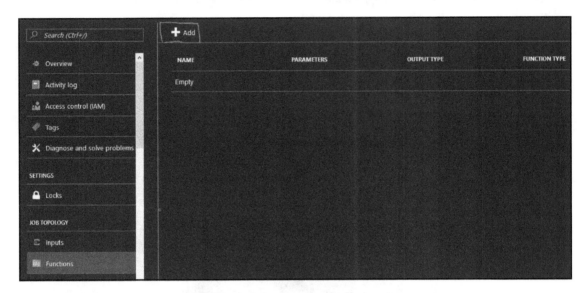

3. A **New function** window will appear in order to provide the function name; under **Function Type**, select default **JavaScript UDF**. The **Output Type** can be chosen as the return type of the JavaScript function. Stream Analytics supports function output types as **datetime, float, any, array, bigint, record, nvarchar (max)**, and so on:

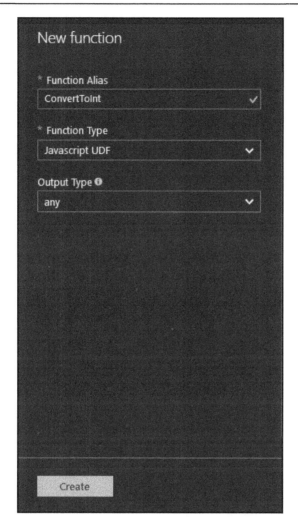

4. A default JavaScript function template will be present, which you may customize. For example, in the following demo, a simple JavaScript UDF function ConvertToInt is provided, which decodes the real-time data streams ingested from Phone accelerometer sensors to Azure Event Hub as hexadecimal to an integer:

```
//UDF to convert Phone Sensor Id from hex to Int
function ConvertToInt(hexVal){
 return Math.round(Number(hexVal)
 );
};
```

5. Save the function in the editor. After saving, it will show **PARAMETERS** equal to 1 and function **OUTPUT TYPE** as **any**:

6. Now, the JavaScript UDF function can be integrated with Stream Analytics query and should be called with the UDF.ConvertToInt alias. So, under **JOB TOPOLOGY**, from the **Query** Tab of Phone sensor data analytics ASA job:

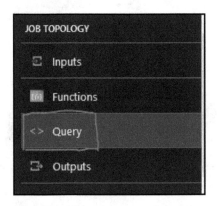

7. The following query should be revised as follows:

```
create table input
(ID BigINT,
Coordinate_X nvarchar(MAX),
Coordinate_Y nvarchar(MAX),
Coordinate_Z nvarchar(MAX))
Select count(input.ID) as SensorID,
UDF.ConvertToInt(input.Coordinate_X) as X_CoOrdinate,
UDF.ConvertToInt(input.Coordinate_Y) as Y_CoOrdinate,
UDF.ConvertToInt(input.Coordinate_Z) as Z_CoOrdinate
into outputblob from input GROUP BY input.Coordinate_X,
input.Coordinate_Y, input.Coordinate_Z,
tumblingWindow(Second,1)
```

In this demo, Event Hub is used to ingest real-time sensor events with X, Y, and Z coordinate values along with SensorID. Then, it is pushed into Stream Analytics to process where the three coordinates complex events values from hexadecimal format are transformed into integers and stored in Azure Blob storage as an output store:

```
09/29/2017 9:58:22 PM> Sending events: {"ID":"601","Coordinate_X":"0.046875","Coordinate_Y":"0.0068359375","Coordinate_Z":"-0.999718070030212"}
09/29/2017 9:58:22 PM> Sending events: {"ID":"602","Coordinate_X":"0.048828125","Coordinate_Y":"0.0078125","Coordinate_Z":"-0.991906642913818"}
09/29/2017 9:58:22 PM> Sending events: {"ID":"603","Coordinate_X":"0.0439453125","Coordinate_Y":"0.0087890625","Coordinate_Z":"-0.994917154312134"}
09/29/2017 9:58:22 PM> Sending events: {"ID":"604","Coordinate_X":"0.0498046875","Coordinate_Y":"0.005859375","Coordinate_Z":"-1.00564444065094"}
09/29/2017 9:58:22 PM> Sending events: {"ID":"605","Coordinate_X":"0.044921875","Coordinate_Y":"0.0048828125","Coordinate_Z":"-0.993041157722473"}
09/29/2017 9:58:22 PM> Sending events: {"ID":"606","Coordinate_X":"0.0498046875","Coordinate_Y":"0.0078125","Coordinate_Z":"-0.996046006679535"}
09/29/2017 9:58:22 PM> Sending events: {"ID":"607","Coordinate_X":"0.048828125","Coordinate_Y":"0.005859375","Coordinate_Z":"-0.997172474861145"}
09/29/2017 9:58:22 PM> Sending events: {"ID":"608","Coordinate_X":"0.05078125","Coordinate_Y":"0.00390625","Coordinate_Z":"-1.00593388080597"}
09/29/2017 9:58:22 PM> Sending events: {"ID":"609","Coordinate_X":"0.048828125","Coordinate_Y":"0.0068359375","Coordinate_Z":"-0.999811589717865"}
09/29/2017 9:58:22 PM> Sending events: {"ID":"610","Coordinate_X":"0.0478515625","Coordinate_Y":"0.005859375","Coordinate_Z":"-1.00235509872437"}
09/29/2017 9:58:22 PM> Sending events: {"ID":"611","Coordinate_X":"0.0439453125","Coordinate_Y":"0.0087890625","Coordinate_Z":"-1.00452327728271"}
09/29/2017 9:58:22 PM> Sending events: {"ID":"612","Coordinate_X":"0.0458984375","Coordinate_Y":"0.0068359375","Coordinate_Z":"-0.999340713024139"}
```

The **Phone Accelerometer** sensor events processed to Azure Service Bus Event Hub:

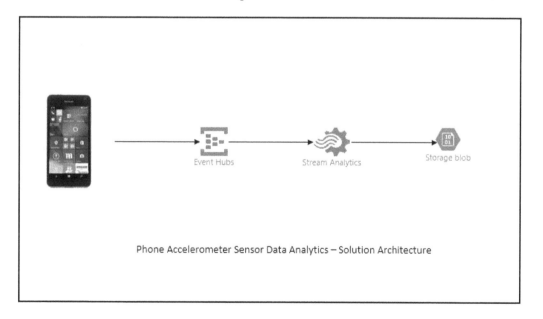

Phone Accelerometer Sensor Data Analytics – Solution Architecture

Stream Analytics and JavaScript data type conversions

While integrating JavaScript functions with Stream Analytics, there are differences in data types that need to be mapped during transformations, such as string datatype in JavaScript, which is converted to `nvarchar (MAX)` in ASA SQL, Object data type in JavaScript to Record type in ASA, Number as BigInt, and Date function to be modified into DateTime in the Stream Analytics Query language. This datatype update specifically requires being taken care of during the selection of **Output Type** of the JavaScript UDF function of Stream Analytics jobs.

Integrating intelligent Azure machine learning algorithms with Stream Analytics function

The Azure Stream Analytics job supports the integration of smart Azure-based machine learning experiments as web services to be consumed as REST API endpoints, invoked as functions. The function can transform the real-time events processed through the Stream Analytics query, invoked through alias and parameters.

In order to define the Azure ML function algorithm with the Stream Analytics function, first the Azure ML experiment should be executed and published as a predictive web service with a REST API endpoint:

1. For Azure Stream Analytics job, in the Azure Portal, under **JOB TOPOLOGY**, select **Functions**.

2. In the **New function** definition window, provide function alias and choose **Azure ML** as the **Function Type**. In the **Import option**, choose either **Select from same subscription** or I**mport from a different subscription** (in case your Azure ML web service resides in a different Azure subscription other than ASA), then provide the Azure ML predictive web service **URL** and **Key**:

3. After adding the Azure ML function, the function alias can be invoked using parameters like `TweetText` with sentiment scores like positive sentiments as 4, neutral sentiments as score 2, and negative as 0. The Azure ML function definition for sentiment scoring of social Twitter feeds collected with specific topics like #**MSIgnite 2017** and #**Azure** consists of sentiment score with `TweetText` as `nvarchar (max)`, and returned as Record datatype in the Stream Analytics function definition:

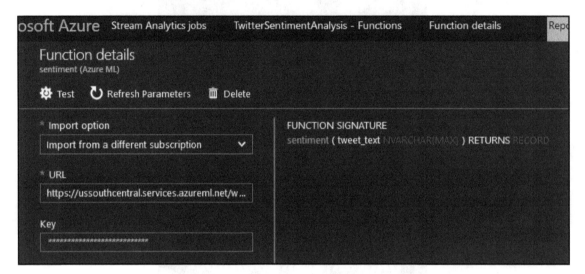

4. In this social sentiment analysis, real-time tweets based on specific keywords have been collected and ingested into the Event Hub to be analyzed and further processed with sentiment ML functions through ASA jobs:

```
WITH subquery AS (
SELECT TweetText, SentimentML(text) as result from input
)
Select TweetText, result.[Scored Labels]
Into outputML
From subquery
```

5. The output of Twitter Sentiment Analytics jobs has been configured with Azure Blob storage and stored as a CSV file where the final processed **TweetText** along with Sentiment Score values are available indicating positive, neutral, or negative tweets:

TweetText	scored labels		
We are chafing the game https://t.co/P4jOWuXtDi	4		
RT @ChrisPatten: Great resources from @_christianWade session today. Excited to get back and show the team! #AzureAnalysisServices¿½		4	
Add Accenture #Cloud Platform 4.0 to #Azure Stack & what do you have? A powerful new tool. #MSIgnite: https://t.co/Ov4SZstUwt		2	
Well good chance we can find you a better job or contract!		2	
.@AVOAcom: Why are enterprises moving away from public cloud? #CIO #cloud #AWS #Azure #GCP https://t.co/8rq7Fyr1qs https://t.co/HhUTcMzRQt			0
RT @msdev_fr: #experiences17 c'est bientï¿½t! 16 #startups (powered by #Azure) seront au village Startup! Inscription gratuiteï¿½			
RT @Sophos: Sophos XG Firewall is on Microsoft #Azure!			
#Decorator #Pattern https://t.co/2ol4CiEcks #javascript #angularjs #nodejs #csharp #dotnet #aws #azure #software #webdevelopment #teachers			2
10 #Microsoft #Azure business benefits in one convenient list https://t.co/BxP5bYUEyK from @RedPixie			2
RT @MSFTAppSource: Discover this app by @SeeqCorporation for #Azure on #MSFTAppSource: https://t.co/8vhldSUCcX https://t.co/hldFdun6O0			2
Frequently asked questions about data protection in #Azure Information Protection	MSFT Docs https://t.co/r90hJkZWGw			2
RT @DataIns8tsCloud: Announcing tools for the #AI-driven #DigitalTransformation			2
Add Accenture #Cloud Platform 4.0 to #Azure Stack & what do you have? A powerful new tool. #MSIgnite: https://t.co/Ov4SZstUwt			2
Add Accenture #Cloud Platform 4.0 to #Azure Stack & what do you have? A powerful new tool. #MSIgnite: https://t.co/Ov4SZstUwt			2

The solution architecture pipeline for Twitter Social Sentiment Analytics is as follows:

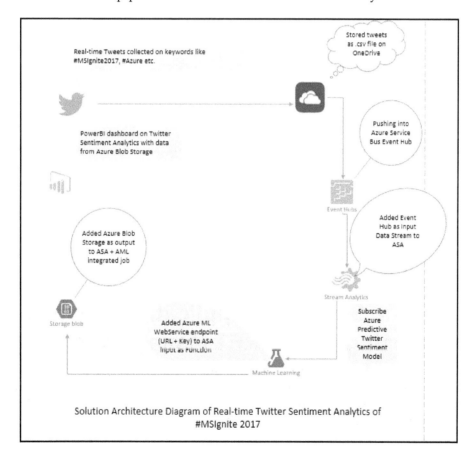

Solution Architecture Diagram of Real-time Twitter Sentiment Analytics of #MSIgnite 2017

- In the Cortana Intelligence gallery, multiple predictive and classification algorithms are available as an experiment, which can be executed with sample data before being published as a **Web service** REST API. For **Twitter sentiments analysis**, a predictive sentiment model is deployed through Azure ML studio, which consists of standard machine learning supervised model experiment process flows like importing data (from Azure Blob storage), data partitioning, and sampling to preprocessing `TweetText` using sample R, then processing through experiment tools such as feature hashing, scoring, and finally being published as a web service output:

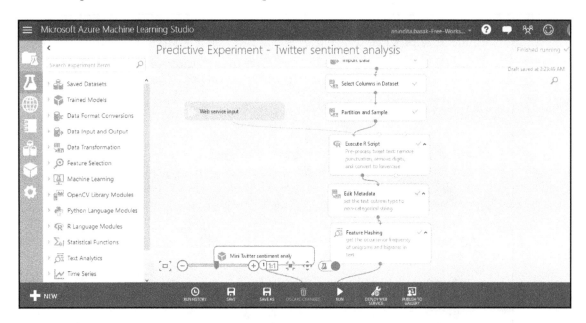

Data pipeline Streaming application building concepts using Azure .NET Management SDK

Azure Stream Analytics jobs provisioning, the configuration of job input, output with query transformation, and starting and stopping of jobs can be managed using Azure .NET SDK with the help of Stream Analytics API. To build Stream Analytics jobs using .NET REST API, the following two class library assemblies are needed:

- `Microsoft.Azure.Management.StreamAnalytics`
- `Microsoft.Azure.Management.StreamAnalytics.Models`

Implementation steps of Azure Stream Analytics jobs using .NET management SDK

To get started with Stream Analytics job provisioning, the configuration of job input, and output and transformation, the prerequisite tools needed are as follows:

- Visual Studio 2017 or 2015 (Enterprise, Professional/Ultimate, or Community Edition)
- Azure .NET SDK 2.7.1 or higher (https://azure.microsoft.com/en-us/downloads/)

Before the development of C# code to provision Azure Stream Analytics jobs using Stream Analytics .NET REST API, the Azure Resource Group needs to be provisioned using PowerShell commands by logging into your Azure account:

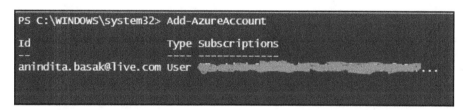

By selecting the appropriate Azure subscription to provision Azure Resource Group in order to deploy ASA jobs using C# .NET REST API, the stream analytics API should be registered with the subscription (if not registered the first time):

```
PS C:\WINDOWS\system32> Register-AzureRMProvider -Force -ProviderNamespace 'Microsoft.StreamAnalytics'
```

The **Azure Resource Group**, which is a container of logical units bound together, consists of Azure resources unified to roll up management, monitoring, and billing details within the same resource group, and assists access to the resources. The resource group is provisioned using REST API with the following command:

```
New-AzureRmResourceGroup -Name <Azure Resource Group Name> -Location <Azure
Resource Group Location>
```

1. Next, create a new C# console project from Visual Studio by choosing **File** | **New** | **Project**, and select C# **Console Application**:

2. Install the **Stream Analytics REST API** class library packages from **NuGet Package Manager** console(**Tools** | **NuGet Package Manager->Package Manager Console**) in order to access the necessary classes and namespaces to provision Stream Analytics jobs:

```
Install-Package Microsoft.Azure.Management.StreamAnalytics -Version
2.0.0
Install-Package Microsoft.Rest.ClientRuntime.Azure.Authentication -
Version 2.3.0
```

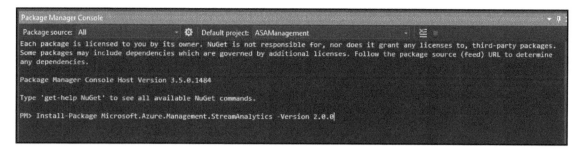

Azure Stream Analytics Management tools installation through NuGet

3. Assign the following application configuration properties in `App.config` by defining `clientid`, `Azure subscription Id`, `active directory tenant id`, and `redirect uri`. The `active directory tenant id` can be found by issuing the following command in the PowerShell command:

```
Login-AzureRmAccount
```

```
PS C:\WINDOWS\system32> Login-AzureRmAccount

Environment            : AzureCloud
Account                : anindita.basak@live.com
TenantId               :
SubscriptionId         :
SubscriptionName       : Visual Studio Enterprise with MSDN
CurrentStorageAccount  :
```

The `ClientId` and `RedirectUri` key parameters are hard-coded and appear by default with the installation of Stream Analytics tools in the value section of `App.config`:

```
<appSettings>
<add key="ClientId" value="<<Client Id of your application>>" />//
<add key="RedirectUri" value="<<Redirect Uri of your application" />
<add key="SubscriptionId" value="<Your Azure Subscription Id>" />
<add key="ActiveDirectoryTenantId" value="<Active Directory Tenant Id>" />
</appSettings>
```

4. Next, start to implement the Stream Analytics job management by first invoking the Azure subscription credentials. Define the following namespaces in the `Program.cs` file:

```
using System;
using System.Collections.Generic;
using System.Linq;
using System.Text;
using System.Threading.Tasks;
using Microsoft.Azure.Management.StreamAnalytics;
using Microsoft.Azure.Management.StreamAnalytics.Models;
using Microsoft.Rest.Azure.Authentication;
using Microsoft.Rest;
using System.Threading;
using System.Configuration;
```

5. Within the `Main` method of the `Program.cs` file, initialize variables for Azure Resource Group name, Stream Analytics job name, job input, output, and transformation name. Define the Azure authentication helper method call signature:

```
string AzureresourceGroupName = "packtdemos"; //<Your Azure
Resource Group Name>
string AzurestreamingJobName = "packtasanetdemo"; // <Your Stream
Analytics job Name>
string ASAinputName = "input";  // <Stream Analytics job Input
Name>
string ASAtransformationName = "asatsql";  // <Stream Analytics Job
Transformation Name>
string ASAoutputName = "output"; //<Stream Analytics Job Output
Name>
```

6. The synchronization context needs to be specified as well using the `SetSynchronizationContent` method and initializing the object:

```
SynchronizationContext.SetSynchronizationContext(new
SynchronizationContext());
```

7. Azure subscription credentials to provision the Stream Analytics job using the REST API need to be defined using the `GetAzureCredentials` method with the `ServiceClientCredentials` class:

```
// Get Azure credentials
ServiceClientCredentials credentials =
GetAzureCredentials().Result;
```

8. The Azure service credentials method is an asynchronous method with the `Task` class. It specifies the Azure authentication helper function block Azure Active Directory client settings, passing parameters of `ClientId` and `ActiveDirectoryTenantId`. Paste the following method next to `Main()` method of `Program.cs` file:

```
private static async Task<ServiceClientCredentials>
GetAzureCredentials()
{
var activeDirectoryClientSettings =
ActiveDirectoryClientSettings.UsePromptOnly(ConfigurationManager.Ap
pSettings["ClientId"], new Uri("urn:ietf:wg:oauth:2.0:oob"));
ServiceClientCredentials credentials = await
UserTokenProvider.LoginWithPromptAsync(ConfigurationManager.AppSett
ings["ActiveDirectoryTenantId"], activeDirectoryClientSettings);
return credentials;
}
```

9. Azure Stream Analytics job creation, specifying job input, output, and transformation is achieved through .NET REST API using the `StreamAnalyticsManagementClient` class, which requires being initialized with the `SubscriptionId`. Write the following code-block next to `GetAzureCredentials()` method invocation of `ServiceClientCredentials` class in `Main()` method:

```
Console.WriteLine("The Stream Analytics job Initialization...");
// Create Stream Analytics management client
StreamAnalyticsManagementClient streamAnalyticsManagementClient =
new StreamAnalyticsManagementClient(credentials)
{
SubscriptionId = ConfigurationManager.AppSettings["SubscriptionId"]
};
```

10. Create the Stream Analytics job next using the `StreamAnalyticsManagementClient` class within the `Main()` method of `Program.cs` file and pass the Azure service credentials object. The `StreamingJob` class helps create the job provision with properties such as job region allocation, `EventsOutOfOrderPolicy`, `OutputErrorPolicy`, `EventLateArrivalMaxDelayInSeconds`, `Sku` definition, and so on:

```
// Create Azure streaming job
 StreamingJob streamingJob = new StreamingJob()
 {
 Tags = new Dictionary<string, string>()
 {
```

```
{ "Origin", ".NET SDK" },
{ "ReasonCreated", "Stream Analytics Job Provision Using .NET
Management SDK" }
},
Location = "East Asia",
EventsOutOfOrderPolicy = EventsOutOfOrderPolicy.Adjust,
EventsOutOfOrderMaxDelayInSeconds = 2,
EventsLateArrivalMaxDelayInSeconds = 16,
OutputErrorPolicy = OutputErrorPolicy.Stop,
DataLocale = "en-US",
CompatibilityLevel = CompatibilityLevel.OneFullStopZero,
Sku = new Sku()
{
Name = SkuName.Standard
}
};
StreamingJob createNewStreamingJobResult =
streamAnalyticsManagementClient.StreamingJobs.CreateOrReplace(strea
mingJob, AzureresourceGroupName, AzurestreamingJobName);
```

11. After defining the ASA job, initialization, next define the job input, output, and transformation with `Main()` method, it should be designed using `Input`, `Output`, and `Transformation` classes available from the `Microsoft.Azure.Management.StreamAnalytics.Models` assembly. Azure Blob storage, Event Hub, or IoT Hub is utilized as a data input stream or reference stream of the Stream Analytics job:

```
Input input = new Input()
{
Properties = new StreamInputProperties()
{
Serialization = new CsvSerialization()
{
FieldDelimiter = ",",
Encoding =
Microsoft.Azure.Management.StreamAnalytics.Models.Encoding.UTF8
},
```

In this demo, Azure Blob storage is used as a job input and is configured with Storage Account API along with defining storage account name, key, container name, path pattern, and date/time format:

```
StorageAccount storageAccount = new StorageAccount()
{
AccountName = "<Your Azure Storage Account Name>",
AccountKey = "<Your Azure Storage Account Key>"
};
```

The Storage Account properties initialize the `BlobStreamInputDataSource` class:

```
Datasource = new BlobStreamInputDataSource()
{
StorageAccounts = new[] { storageAccount },
Container = "asatelemetry",
PathPattern = "{date}/{time}",
DateFormat = "yyyy/MM/dd",
TimeFormat = "HH",
SourcePartitionCount = 16
}
```

12. The input data source credentials can also be verified using the `ResourceTestStatus` class with the definition of the `Test` method passing the Azure resource group name, streaming job name, and ASA job input name:

```
Input createInputResult =
streamAnalyticsManagementClient.Inputs.CreateOrReplace(input,
AzureresourceGroupName, AzurestreamingJobName, ASAinputName);
 // Test the connection to the input
 ResourceTestStatus testInputResult =
streamAnalyticsManagementClient.Inputs.Test(AzureresourceGroupName,
AzurestreamingJobName, ASAinputName);
```

13. The `Output` class defines the job output configuration. The Azure SQL database is used as an ASA job output in this demo and the `Transformation` class is initialized to create an object to pass through the ASA SQL job query, which can be passed through C#. The `AzureSqlDatabaseOutputDataSource` API defines the object to pass the SQL DB properties like server name, database name and credentials, table definition, and so on:

```
// Create an output
 Output output = new Output()
 {
 Datasource = new AzureSqlDatabaseOutputDataSource()
 {
 Server = "<Azure SQL db>.database.windows.net",
 Database = "<Azure SQL db Name>",
 User = "<Database User>",
 Password = "<Database Password>",
 Table = "<Database Table Name>"
 }
 };
 Output createOutputResult =
streamAnalyticsManagementClient.Outputs.CreateOrReplace(output,
AzureresourceGroupName, AzurestreamingJobName, ASAoutputName);
```

The `Transformation` **class definition to configure the ASA job query is as follows:**

```
// Create a transformation
Transformation transformation = new Transformation()
{
Query = "Select Id, Name, JobCode from input", // 'Query' is fully
customizable as per as required for ASA job
StreamingUnits = 1  // SU defines the job compute capacity with respect to
CPU, memory, data processing throughput
};
Transformation createTransformationResult =
streamAnalyticsManagementClient.Transformations.CreateOrReplace(transformat
ion, AzureresourceGroupName, AzurestreamingJobName, ASAtransformationName);
```

14. Finally, the job starts and stop options can be implemented using the start and stop methods of the `StreamAnalyticsManagementClient` class. This job starts and stopping definition is designed using a wrapper object of the `StartStreamingJobParameters` API:

```
// Start a streaming job
StartStreamingJobParameters startStreamingJobParameters = new
StartStreamingJobParameters()
{
OutputStartMode = OutputStartMode.CustomTime,
OutputStartTime = new DateTime(2012, 12, 12, 12, 12, 12,
DateTimeKind.Utc)
};
streamAnalyticsManagementClient.StreamingJobs.Start(AzureresourceGr
oupName, AzurestreamingJobName, startStreamingJobParameters);
Console.WriteLine("The Stream Analytics job has been started....");
// Stop a streaming job
streamAnalyticsManagementClient.StreamingJobs.Stop(AzureresourceGro
upName, AzurestreamingJobName);
Console.WriteLine("The Stream Analytics job has stopped...");
```

15. Similarly, the provisioned job could be deleted by invoking the delete method of the `StreamAnalyticsManagementClient` object:

```
streamAnalyticsManagementClient.StreamingJobs.Delete(resourceGroupN
ame, streamingJobName)
```

16. While the Stream Analytics job is undergoing provision, its status can be monitored using the Azure portal. The program should be executed by clicking on the **Start** button or pressing *F5*. It will prompt you to enter your Azure account credentials for the first time and then the job will be in the starting state to running state and finally stopped state in an automated manner using the .NET management API observed through the Azure portal:

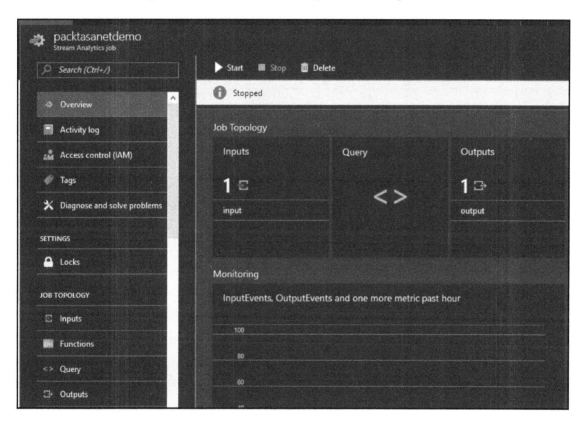

Summary

In this chapter, you learned about enhancing Stream Analytics real-time event processing queries, optimized through integrating with JavaScript functions for data transformation, mathematical or statistical analysis purposes, and applying intelligent predictive algorithms using Azure machine learning web services with interactive data streams. Finally, step-by-step implementation guidance was analyzed to build a Stream Analytics job with customized input, output, and job transformation, and starting and stopping phases using the .NET REST API.

In the next chapter, we will focus on understanding the Stream Analytics job monitoring and management processes using job diagram metrics, resource health enhancement, diagnostics log collection for troubleshooting, and architectural principles of designing optimized job monitoring concepts.

10
Understanding Stream Analytics Job Monitoring

When it comes to streaming data analytics, achieving shorter action times and insights is extremely important. A few minutes of service downtime can be extremely expensive for mission-critical applications and can impact on your business. In scenarios where you may have less than a second to identify and stop a fraudulent credit card transaction before it goes through, raise an alert based on a health event from a device monitoring the vitals of a patient, or halt an overheated engine before it results in major damage, service availability and uptime are of the highest importance. Hence, in comparison to the traditional world of batch analytics, you may not have the luxury of time to troubleshoot issues or perform root cause analysis when something goes wrong, or an unexpected event happens.

With that said, let's explore some of the key monitoring and diagnosis features provided by Azure, and understand how they can save you a ton of time and effort when it comes to diagnosing and troubleshooting unexpected issues or events with your Stream Analytics jobs. This will equip you better the next time you run into issues, such as jobs not outputting data, consuming too many SUs, or if there is a backlog of unprocessed events.

Azure provides the following monitoring capabilities for Stream Analytics jobs:

- Job metrics
- Job diagrams
- Diagnostics logs
- Alerts to send notifications and take actions for critical events
- Integration with third-party monitoring and alerting applications

Let's look at each of these capabilities in the following couple of sections.

Troubleshooting with job metrics

All Azure services (including Stream Analytics) emit several metrics that can provide rich insights into the performance, usage, and health of different components. In the case of a Stream Analytics job, job metrics provide valuable information that let you track job operations and understand what's going on with a job. The metrics are generated out-of-the-box; you don't need to do anything to create these. You can, however, choose metrics of interest from the list of available metrics and also pin them to a dashboard for monitoring. Apart from the Azure portal, metrics can also be accessed programmatically through REST APIs and .NET SDK.

Follow the following steps to browse the available metrics for your Stream Analytics job:

1. Log in to the Azure portal.
2. Navigate to your Stream Analytics job.
3. Examine the metrics on the chart under the **Monitoring** section as shown in the following screenshot, *Monitoring Job Metrics for a Stream Analytics job*. The chart shows the following key metrics for the past hour:
    - **Input Events**: Amount of data (number of events) received by the job
    - **Output Events**: Amount of data (number of events) sent to the output

- **Runtime Errors**: Errors during job execution

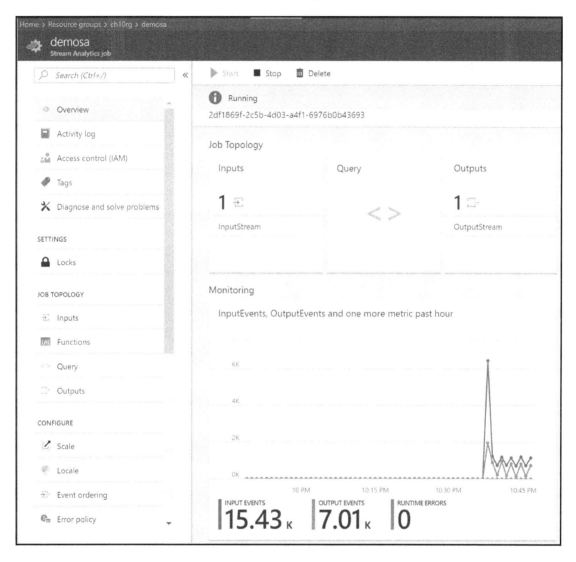

Monitoring job metrics for a Stream Analytics job

4. The chart can be easily modified to display further information according to your needs. Click on the monitoring chart to launch a modification dialogue with options to edit the chart and define alerts, as shown in the following screenshot:

Modification dialogue for the Stream Analytics monitoring chart

5. Hit the **Edit chart** button to get a list of additional metrics that can be added to the chart, as shown in the following figure. You can customize the following items on the chart:

- **Chart type**: Choose from **Bar** or **Line** chart
- **Time range**: Choose from an existing option or specify your own
- **Metrics**: Add or remove metrics. The three metrics precedingly discussed are already selected:

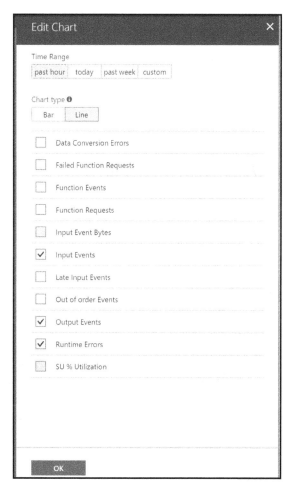

Editing the metric chart

6. Hit the **OK** button to save any changes.

The preceding screenshot shows different metrics available for monitoring. Let's look at each of these, and understand what information is captured and presented by the respective metric:

- **Data Conversion Errors**: Keeps track of the count of data conversion errors during the job execution
- **Failed Function Requests**: Count on failed **Azure Machine Learning (AML)** function requests
- **Function Requests**: Count of events the AML function calls
- **Input Event Bytes**: Bytes of input data received by the job
- **Input Events**: Number of input events received by the job can be used for determining if the job is receiving input data
- **Late Input Events**: Input events arriving late from the source
- **Out of order Events**: Input events received out of order
- **Output Events**: Number of output events sent to output by the job
- **Runtime Errors**: Count of errors encountered during job execution
- **SU % Utilization**: Indicator of resource utilization. In percentage, the measure of **Streaming Units (SUs)** utilized by the job

Visual monitoring of job diagram

Job metrics have been around for a while and provide a bunch of metrics for errors, inputs, outputs, and resource utilization. Job diagram takes it to the next level and provides advanced job monitoring capabilities, allowing you to monitor and troubleshoot your job in a more visual manner. A Stream Analytics job is broken down into logical constructs based on the job definition and the query steps, and a visual representation of steps is provided in terms of inputs, outputs, and individual query steps. You can hover over and click on each step for more information and also get the code associated with the specific step. The diagram also provides a timeline of events with information, such as the number of input events coming in, the total number of events going out, and so on, plotted on the timeline chart.

The central theme behind job diagrams is that in case of an issue, a visual representation of job steps can help speed up isolation of the issue to a specific job step. Hovering over and clicking on individual sub-steps lets you examine key metrics quickly and identify the problematic piece. You can also view the code associated with a step in the side panel, and troubleshoot the logic implemented.

Follow the following steps to view the job diagram for your Stream Analytics job:

1. Select **Job diagram** under **SUPPORT + TROUBLESHOOTING,** as shown in the following screenshot:

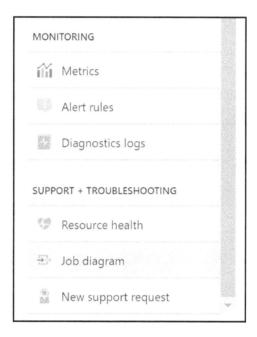

Viewing job diagram for a Stream Analytics job

2. This should bring up the **Job diagram** for your Stream Analytics job, as shown in the following screenshot. Hover over different steps to view job metrics for the step, or the underlying query associated with the step:

Troubleshooting with a Stream Analytics job diagram

3. Hover over a query step to view the underlying query associated with the step. The following screenshot illustrates a step with the associated query, outputting data to a Power BI sink:

Viewing a query associated with a step

4. You can also view the metrics for individual partitions. Hit the **Expand all** button in the top-left corner, as shown in the following screenshot, to expand all partitions. Select a partition to filter the chart at the bottom, only for the selected partition:

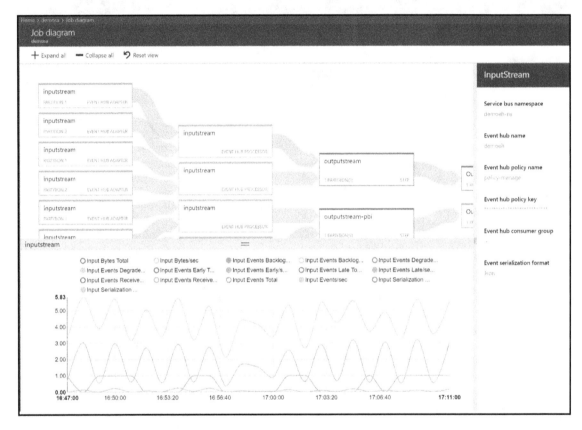

Viewing metrics for a partition

As an example, let's click an input job step in the job diagram and hover over the timeline chart to examine some of the input metrics displayed at a point in time, as shown in the following screenshot:

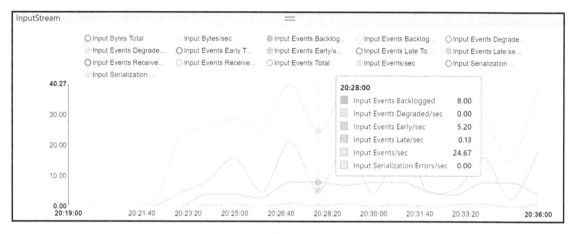

Examining metrics displayed in the timeline chart

The following are some types of issues that can be identified with the help of input metrics, shown in the preceding screenshot:

Determine if the job is receiving input events:

- **Input Events/sec**

Events indicating any errors in input data:

- **Input Serialization Errors/sec**
- **Input Events Degraded/sec**

Determine if any events arrived out of order from the source, or are backlogged:

- **Input Events Backlogged**
- **Input Events Early/sec**
- **Input Events Late/sec**

Logging of diagnostics logs

Azure diagnostics logs are another great troubleshooting mechanism to get information about the operation of an Azure resource—a Stream Analytics job in our case. Let's understand how the information provided by diagnostics logs can help you to troubleshoot issues faster, in case of an unexpected event. You can use diagnostics logs to collect the following categories of data:

- **Execution**: Log events occurring at runtime, that is, during job execution
- **Authoring**: Capturing job authoring events, such as job creation/modification
- **All Metrics**: Log metrics emitted by a Stream Analytics job

When it comes to storage and consumption of diagnostics logs, you have the following three options at hand:

- **Archive to a storage account**: You can choose to store the diagnostics logs on a storage account for later analysis, or for auditing purposes. When a storage account is chosen as an option, you can optionally specify a retention period (in days) for the logs. A retention period configuration of zero implies the logs will be retained forever.
- **Stream to an Event Hub**: You can also stream the diagnostics logs to Event Hub. This is very useful, involving integration with a third-party monitoring/log analytics application, or even visualizing log data in Power BI.
- **Send to Log Analytics**: It is a service part of Microsoft's **Operations Management Suite (OMS)**, and provides a central repository for data related to monitoring and performance events for your Azure and on-premises environments. Diagnostics logs can be sent to Log Analytics, which makes it available for further analysis, visualizations, and alerting.

Enabling diagnostics logs

Diagnostics logs are disabled by default. Follow the following steps to enable diagnostics logs for your job:

1. Log in to the Azure portal and navigate to your Stream Analytics job

2. Select the **Diagnostics logs** blade under the **MONITORING** section, and click on the **Turn on diagnostics** link in the corresponding pane on the right, as shown in the following screenshot:

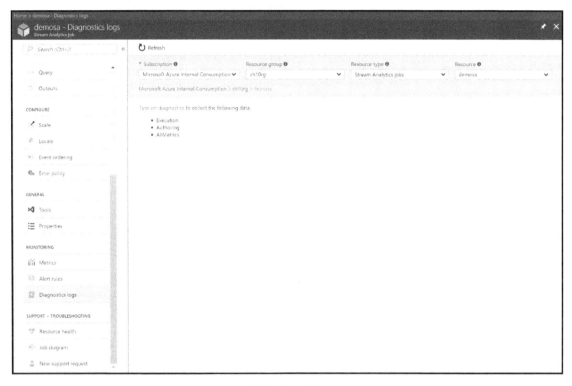

Enabling diagnostics logs

3. For the sake of this example, let's send the **Execution** and **Authoring** logs to a storage account. To achieve this, configure the following options, as shown in the following screenshot:
   1. Provide a name for the logs
   2. Configure the destination storage account

3. Select the **Execution** and **Authoring** checkboxes:

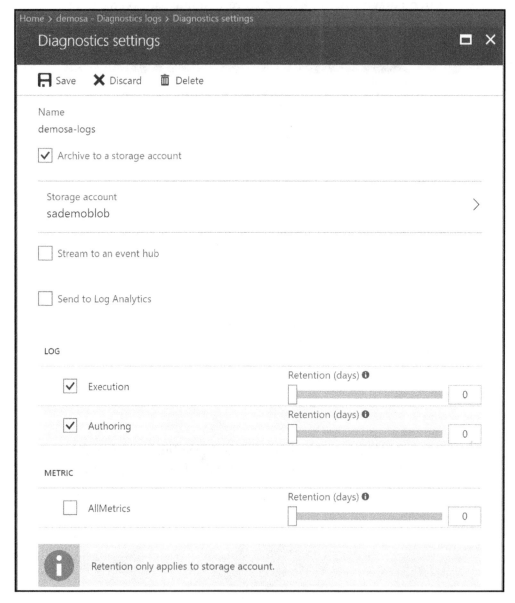

Sending diagnostics logs to a storage account

4. Hit the **Save** button after performing the configurations in the previous step

Exploring the logs sent to the storage account

Once the logs are enabled, you can use tools such as **Azure Storage Explorer** to explore the diagnostics logs generated by the Stream Analytics job. Follow the following steps to access the diagnostics logs generated by the job:

1. Launch Azure Storage Explorer
2. Log in to your Azure account and locate the storage account you configured as the destination for the diagnostics logs
3. Look for `insights-logs-authoring` and `insights-logs-execution` containers, as shown in the following screenshot:

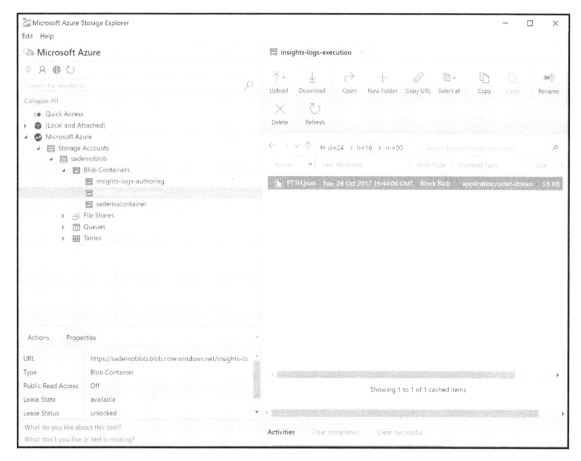

Exploring logs sent to the storage accounts

4. Navigate to the lowest level in the `insights-logs-execution` subfolder, and examine the contents of the JSON file. Logs within the container follow the following storage pattern:

```
insights-logs-
{logcategory}/resourceId=/{resourceId}/y={year}/m={month}/d=
{day}/h={24-hour}/m=00/PT1H.json
```

5. Examine the contents of the log file. The following screenshot shows informational events such as stopping the job, job validation, and so on, logged as individual records in a JSON file:

Examining the contents of an execution log

Configuring job alerts

Getting insights using job metrics and diagnostics logs is crucial for job monitoring and troubleshooting issues. However, it would take an enormous amount of human effort to keep a watch on various metrics 24/7 and raise an alarm or take immediate action in case of any issues. Hence, another important aspect of job monitoring is letting the platform do the hard work of monitoring, notifying a human, or performing a custom action when a metric reaches a critical threshold. The Azure alert experience fills this gap and provides a highly intuitive experience for setting up job alerts to take an action when a job metric reaches a predefined threshold.

Let's understand the features offered with an example. To ensure that your Stream Analytics job processes incoming events with low latency, you may want to keep an eye on the job's resource consumption. One way to accomplish this is by setting an alert on the SU% utilization metric. Apart from sending an email notification, you can also tie-up an alert to a webhook. A webhook allows you to take a custom action on an alert, such as sending an SMS or directing an alert to another alert subsystem for further processing.

Follow the following steps to send out an email in case the metric goes beyond the 80% threshold:

1. Navigate to your Azure Stream Analytics job in the Azure portal
2. Click on the **Monitoring** section of the **Overview** blade
3. Click on the **Add alert** button, as shown in the following screenshot, to create a new alert:

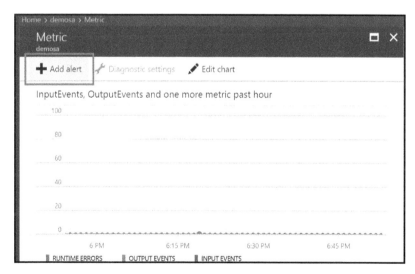

Adding an alert rule

4. Provide a **Name** and **Description** of the new alert. Also specify the **Metric** of interest, **Condition**, and **Threshold** values to trigger an action (email notification, in this example), as shown in the following screenshot:

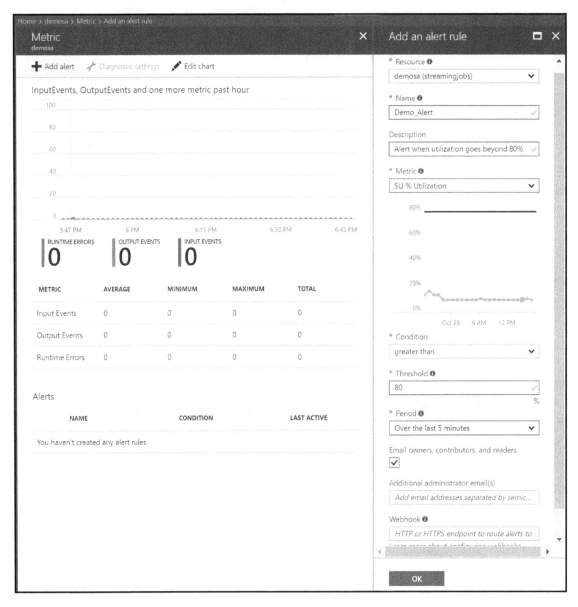

Creating an alert to monitor the SU % Utilization metric

5. Hit the **OK** button to create the new alert rule.

Anytime the SU % utilization metric goes beyond the configured threshold of 80%, an alert will be generated and an email notification will be sent out.

Viewing resource health information with Azure resource health

Resource health history is another Azure feature that can help you save time on issue diagnosis by providing up to 14 days of historical health information for an Azure resource. Resource health keeps an eye on your Azure resources, a Stream Analytics job in our case, to ensure that everything is working as expected and provides information on any Azure service issues leading to downtime of your Azure resources. The following are different types of health statuses reported by resource health:

- **Available**: As the name suggests, there aren't any known issues with the resource, and the resource is available
- **Unavailable**: Indicates a problem and unavailability of the resource
- **Unknown**: Resource health is not able to determine the status of the resource

Based on the status of the resource and underlying issue, Azure resource health provides more information on the issue to help you save on troubleshooting time and effort.

You can view the resource health for your Stream Analytics job by clicking on the **Resource health** blade under **SUPPORT + TROUBLESHOOTING** on the Azure portal, as shown in the following screenshot:

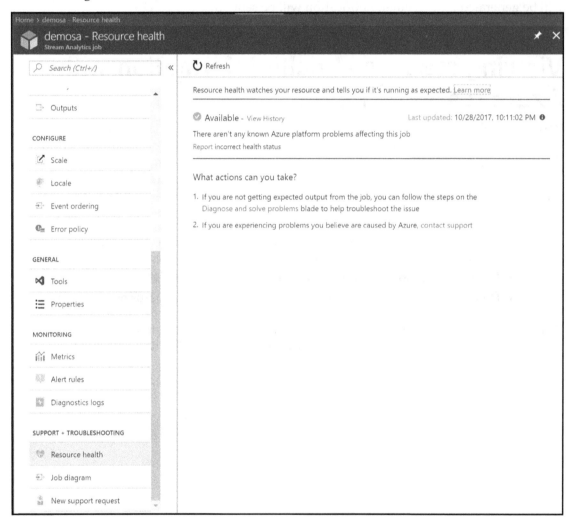

Viewing resource health information

You can also hit the **History** button to view up to 14 days of historical resource health information, as shown in the following screenshot:

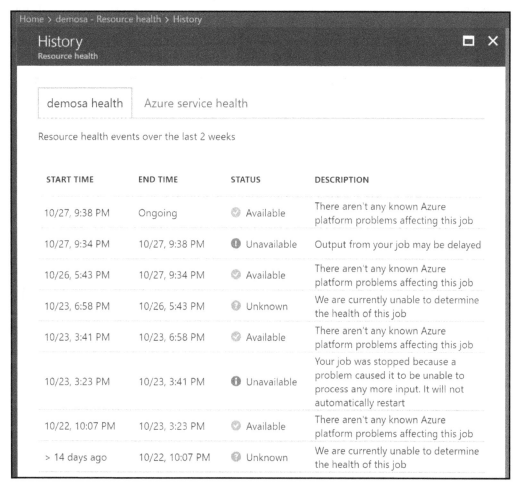

Exploring historical resource health information

If you believe that the current health of the Azure resource (as reported by **Resource health**) is not correct, you also have the option of reporting an incorrect status, as shown in the earlier figure, *Viewing resource health information*. You can also look at the list of common issues for the resources and steps to resolve them by hitting the **Diagnose and solve problems** link. For example, the following screenshot shows some of the common problems associated with Stream Analytics jobs and steps to troubleshoot the issues:

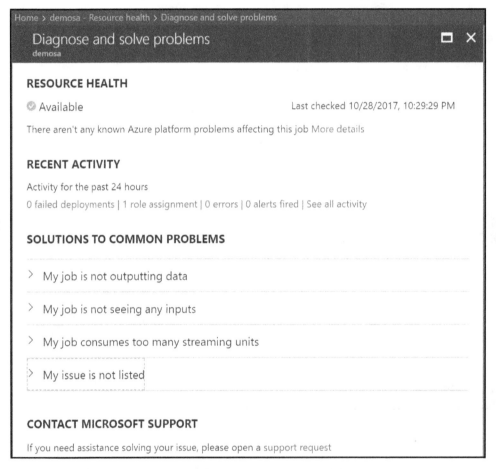

Solutions to common problems related to Stream Analytics jobs

Microsoft also recommends reaching out for support through the **Resource health** blade if you need assistance with an issue because of a problem with an Azure Service.

Exploring different monitoring experiences

So far, we have looked at monitoring experiences in the context of the Azure portal. The following are some of the other options for working with the Azure monitoring experience, apart from the Azure portal:

- **REST APIs**: Azure monitor REST APIs let you retrieve definitions and values for metrics, logs, and alerts programmatically using REST APIs. Developers can consume these APIs in their custom applications, or retrieve and save the data in data stores for further analysis.
- **PowerShell**: You can also use PowerShell cmdlets to access metrics and monitoring information
- **Cross-platform CLI**: You can also access Azure monitoring features via the Azure CLI. In case you are not familiar with the Azure CLI (command-line interface), it is Azure's new cross-platform command-line experience that you can use in your browser with Azure Cloud Shell, or you can install it on macOS, Linux, and Windows, and run it from the command line.
- **SDKs**: Azure SDKs, available for different languages and platforms of your choice, can also be used for monitoring Azure resources. SDKs are available for languages such as .NET, Java, Python, and so on, different platforms.

As an example, let's look at the PowerShell experience and try to access job metrics using Azure PowerShell. The PowerShell cmdlet `Get-AzureRmMetric` can be used to get metrics for a given Azure resource. The cmdlet requires the following parameters:

- `ResourceId`: Fully qualified ID of the Stream Analytics job, which includes the Azure subscription ID, resource group name, and resource name (name of the Stream Analytics job)
- `MetricNames`: Name of the job metric (`Input events`, in this example)
- `TimeGrain`: Time grain for the metric in the format hh: mm: ss
- `StartTime`: Time from which metric data will be retrieved
- `EndTime`: End time to which metric data will be retrieved

The following PowerShell command retrieves the value of the Input Events metric every 1 hour for the previous 4 hours, as shown in the screenshot, *Retrieving job metrics with PowerShell*:

```
(Get-AzureRmMetric -ResourceId
"/subscriptions/<<subscriptionid>>/resourceGroups/ch10rg/providers/Microsof
t.StreamAnalytics/streamingjobs/<<jobname>>" -TimeGrain "01:00:00" -
StartTime (get-date).AddHours(-4) -EndTime (get-date) -MetricNames
"InputEvents").data | Format-table -wrap Timestamp,Total
```

The output is as follows:

Retrieving job metrics with PowerShell

Furthermore, to get a list of supported metrics by the Azure resource, the Get-AzureRmMetricDefinition cmdlet can be used. The following PowerShell command describes an example of invoking the function using the fully-qualified resource name as the parameter:

```
Get-AzureRmMetricDefinition -ResourceId
"/subscriptions/<<subscriptionid>>/resourceGroups/ch10rg/providers/Microsof
t.StreamAnalytics/streamingjobs/<<jobname>>"
```

Building a monitoring dashboard

The Azure monitoring experience provides users with rich monitoring and diagnostics features, enabling them to monitor different components of their solution in one place. Most of the monitoring feature discussed in this chapter (job metrics, diagnostics logs, resource health, and alerts) are platform features and can be set up to monitor other Azure resources as well in a similar fashion.

Any real-world solution would include a plethora of Azure resources belonging to different Azure services working in conjunction to achieve the solution's objectives. Without the platform level monitoring features, it can become a nightmare to monitor all the different solution components for performance issues and errors. Azure lets you pin monitoring visuals and views them from different resources to a build a comprehensive solution monitoring dashboard, as shown in the following screenshot:

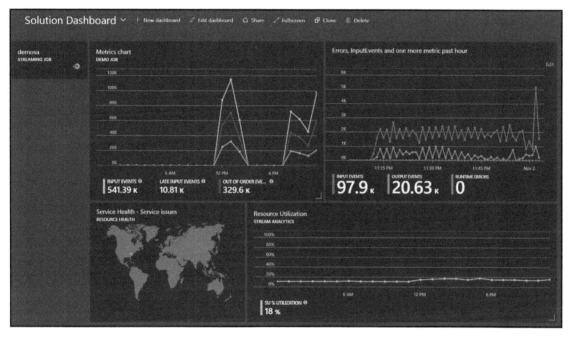

Building a monitoring dashboard

The dashboard in the preceding figure can be extended by including similar views from other components of your solution to provide a holistic view of your application. This is the key to monitoring your Azure environment.

Summary

In this chapter, we learnt about troubleshooting with job metrics and visual monitoring of job diagrams. We also explored the logging of diagnostic logs along, and also how to enable diagnostic logs. Also, we understood how to view resource health information using Azure resource health.

In the next chapter, we will be going through different use cases for real-world data stream architectures.

11

Use Cases for Real-World Data Streaming Architectures

Real-world streaming architectures and event processing applications have been adopted by most data-driven companies around today. In order to gain some insight into low latency data, the processing of the data stream is important. This may be in the form of continuous streaming of events such as GPS signals, human heartbeats, ocean currents, weather sensor information, social media feeds, and so on. Stream-based, real-time architectures provide fundamental and powerful advantages, not just for utilizing in highly-specialized projects, but also in stream-based computing. They are becoming the norm for data-driven enterprises, and this allows them to efficiently implement new, flexible, and technical architectural designs and creates scalable, optimized models for efficient processing of complex business logic.

In this chapter, we'll be focusing on:

- Designing a solution architecture for a case study—building social media sentiment analytics using Twitter and a real-time sentiment analytics dashboard
- Remote monitoring analytics using Azure IoT Suite with streaming data
- Connected factory solutions, dominantly used in Industrie 4.0 using Azure IoT Suite
- Real-world telecom fraud detection analytics using Azure Streaming and Cortana Intelligence Gallery, with interactive visuals from Microsoft Power BI

Over the past few decades, multiple industries have experienced the value of transformation. These include the automotive, manufacturing, retail, and financial industries. They are driven by competition in order to innovate and optimize their business through digital transformation using platforms such as the **Internet of Things** (**IoT**), industrial IoT, economic IoT, and consumer IoT. As businesses start to build on their complex, competitive advantages with operations such as fleet management, anomaly detection, predictive analytics, remote monitoring, connected cars, connected factories, and so on, their need for processing and analytics of those real-time smart data streams increases.

Solution architecture design and Proof-of-Concept implementation of social media sentiment analytics using Twitter and a sentiment analytics dashboard

In order to transform and extract Real-Time Insights from complex events for making key operational decisions, we will use Azure Stream Analytics. By uncovering the power of data insights coming from social media feeds, posts, weblogs, and clickstream event logs, we are able to then utilize these insights to build rich visuals, webhook alerts, or trigger workflows. In this demo, step-by-step guidance is provided in order to design a solution architecture and implement social sentiment analytics using Twitter with Azure Stream Analytics and the Azure analytical platform stack.

Definition of sentiment analytics

Sentiment analytics is defined as the identification of opinions regarding a particular product, incident, or event in terms of positive, negative, or neutral mood posts. This is also known as opinion mining and is collected from social feeds and analyzed through a real-time, managed streaming engine such as Stream Analytics. In this demo, we have used specific keywords with hashtags such as #**Azure**, #**MSFT**, #**IoT**, #**Office365**, #**Windows10**, and so on, to analyze sentiment detection along percentage analysis in terms of positive, negative, or neutral mood attitudes with the Azure analytics stack.

The following resources are utilized for the implementation of Twitter sentiment analytics using the Azure data platform:

- Azure WebJobs (Python script)
- Azure Service Bus Event Hub (as data stream)
- Azure Blob storage
- Azure Stream Analytics
- Azure Machine Learning workspace
- Power BI Office 365 account
- Azure Functions (optional)

The solution architecture is as shown:

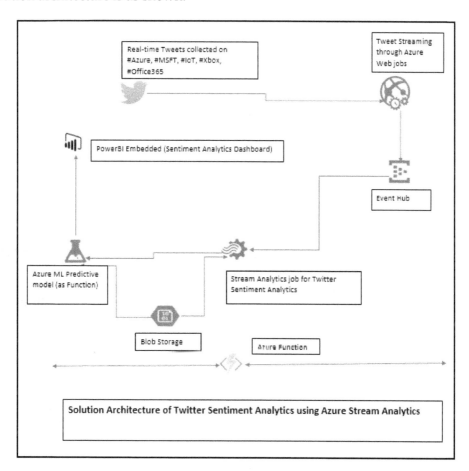

Prerequisites required for the implementation of Twitter sentiment analytics PoC

The prerequisites needed are:

- An Azure subscription
- A Twitter account
- A Twitter application
- Twitter streaming API auth credentials—keys and access tokens, consumer key (API key), and consumer secret (API secret) available from the Twitter application settings
- Python 2.7 and pip
- Tweetpy (`https://github.com/tweepy/tweepy`)(used in this demo)
- Power BI Office 365 account
- Azure Machine Learning workspace

Steps for implementation of Twitter sentiment analytics

In order to build the solution for Twitter sentiment analytics, the first step is to create a Twitter application using your Twitter account credentials:

1. Go to **Twitter Application Management** to create a new app at `https://apps.twitter.com/app/new`. Provide details such as **app name**, **description**, **website,** or **callback url** (optional).

2. On creation of the Twitter app, there will be an option for the application to collect keys and tokens; select **Keys** and **Access Tokens** from the tab and check the **Consumer** Key and **Secret** along with **Access Token** and **Token Secret** values. Copy the values into a text editor to make a note of them, since these values will be needed to create the Twitter streaming simulator application:

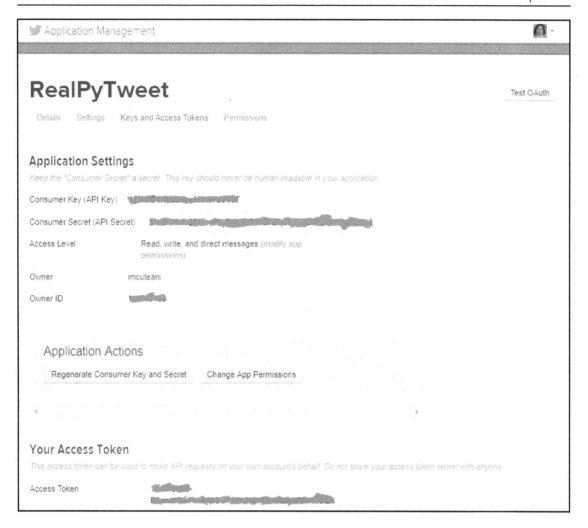

3. Install **Python 2.7 SDK** for Windows by downloading the latest version (2.7.14 at the time of writing) from `https://www.python.org/downloads/windows/`. Install the `pip` package for Python as well so we can use the TweetPy library for collecting real-time tweets based on specific keywords or hashtags. `pip` can be installed after installation of Python. Navigate to the directory (`C:\Python27\Scripts`) and execute `pip.exe`.

4. Next, install TweetPy by typing the following command at the Command Prompt:

```
pip install tweetpy
```

The output of the preceding code is as follows:

Next, create the Twitter streaming simulator using the TweetPy API for collecting real-time tweets using specific keyword hashtags and streaming to the Azure Event Hub. The libraries can be from core Python packages such as os, sys, json, and re along with TweetPy libraries such as Stream, OAuthHandler, StreamListener, and including the Service Bus API. In this simulator, a Python class is defined as a listener inherited from the StreamListener class with Azure Service Bus Event Hub connection string defined. There are multiple functions in this Python-based Twitter data simulator app used for tasks such as initialization, data loading, topics collection, error handling, and finally, Twitter application keywords. So, the first section of the Twitter streaming code block looks as follows:

```
import sys, os, json, re
  from tweepy import Stream                    //TweetPy package declaration
  from tweepy import OAuthHandler
  from tweepy.streaming import StreamListener
  from azure.servicebus import ServiceBusService        // Azure Service
```

```
Bus API
class listener(StreamListener):
 whitespace_regex = re.compile('\s+')
 connection_string_regex =
re.compile('^Endpoint=sb://(.+).servicebus.windows.net/;SharedAccessKeyName
=(.+);SharedAccessKey=(.+);EntityPath=(.+)$')                    // Azure
Event Hub Connection String
 def __init__(self, event_hub_connection_string, keywords):
 m = self.connection_string_regex.match(event_hub_connection_string)
 self.sbs = ServiceBusService(
 m.group(1),
 shared_access_key_name=m.group(2),
 shared_access_key_value=m.group(3))
 self.keywords = keywords
 self.event_hub_name = m.group(4)
```

Next, we need to define the data loading function in Python, where the collected raw tweets will be parsed using the Python JSON library. They will parse, trim whitespaces, add regex expressions, and finally, process them based on specific keywords such as Tweet Text, timestamp, id, retweet_count, timezone, tweet_language, and so on:

```
def on_data(self, data):
 try:
 tweet = json.loads(data)
 p = re.compile('\s+')
 text =tweet['text']
 for topic in self.get_topics(text, keywords):                // loop with
tweet keywords & texts
 output = json.dumps(
 {
 'text': text,                           // Tweet Text
 'timestamp_ms': tweet['timestamp_ms'],  // Tweet Timestamp
 'topic': topic,                         // Tweet Topic
 'id': tweet['id'],                      // Tweet Id
 'retweet_count': tweet['retweet_count'], // retweet Count
 'time_zone': tweet['user']['time_zone'], // Tweet Language
 'lang': tweet['user']['lang']
 })
 self.sbs.send_event(self.event_hub_name, output)     // Ingestion of Tweet
events into Event Hub
 return True
 except BaseException as e:
 print('failed ondata' + str(e))
 time.sleep(5)
def on_error(self, status):
 print(status)
```

In this Twitter simulator app code, we utilized functions with arguments. For example, taking input tweet text with selected keywords such as #Azure, #IoT, and so on. We used the `sanitize_text` function to apply a regular expression to convert all tweet text into lowercase format:

```
def get_topics(self, input, keywords):
return [keyword for keyword in self.keywords if self.sanitize_text(keyword)
in self.sanitize_text(input)]
def sanitize_text(self, input):
return self.whitespace_regex.sub(' ', input.strip().lower())
```

In the final section of the Twitter streaming simulator, we defined the Twitter app settings, configuration values, such as **Twitter OAuth consumer key**, **consumer secret**, **OAuth token**, and **OAuth token secret** values along with Twitter keywords, and passed them into the Stream function of `twitterStream`:

```
keywords = os.environ["TWITTER_KEYWORDS"].split(",")
consumer_key_setting = os.environ["TWITTER_APP_OAUTH_CONSUMER_KEY"]
consumer_secret_setting = os.environ["TWITTER_APP_OAUTH_CONSUMER_SECRET"]
oauth_token_setting = os.environ["TWITTER_APP_OAUTH_TOKEN"]
oauth_token_secret_setting = os.environ["TWITTER_APP_OAUTH_TOKEN_SECRET"]
 # TODO: need to fix connection string types in AzureFunctionApp. Using
AzureSQLCONNSTR_ for now,
 # which is what they all default to.
 # event_hub_connection_string =
os.environ["CUSTOMCONNSTR_EventHubConnectionString"]
event_hub_connection_string =
os.environ["ServiceBus_EventHubConnectionString"]
auth = OAuthHandler(consumer_key_setting, consumer_secret_setting)
auth.set_access_token(oauth_token_setting, oauth_token_secret_setting)
twitterStream = Stream(auth, listener(event_hub_connection_string,
keywords))
twitterStream.filter(track=keywords)
```

This Twitter streaming simulator app sends real-time tweets directly to Event Hub and processes them into a Stream Analytics job. So, make sure to pass the appropriate Event Hub connection string in the simulator app code. The connection string of Event Hub can be found in the Azure portal. Under **Settings,** select **Shared Access policies,** then click on the default **Policy**, such as **RootManageSharedAccessKey** and select its connection string—**Primary key:**

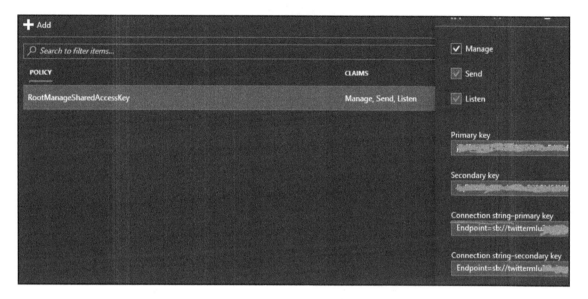

Create the Azure Stream Analytics job from the Azure portal and add the **Twitter Stream Event Hub** as an input data stream from the job topology. When adding the corresponding Twitter Streaming Event Hub as an input for the Stream Analytics job, the appropriate **Event hub policy name**, **policy key**, and **serialization format** need to be declared:

The detailed step of creation of Azure Stream Analytics job is already covered in `Chapter 4`, *Developing Real-Time Event Processing with Azure Streaming* of this book

Now, in order to extract sentiment associated with the collected tweet text from specific keywords, we require the help of an Azure Machine Learning function executed as the predictive analytics web service model. In Azure ML studio (`https://studio.azureml.net`), open the *Predictive Experiment- Mini Twitter sentiment analysis* experiment from the Cortana Intelligence gallery, available at `https://gallery.cortanaintelligence.com/Experiment/Predictive-Mini-Twitter-sentiment-analysis-Experiment-1`:

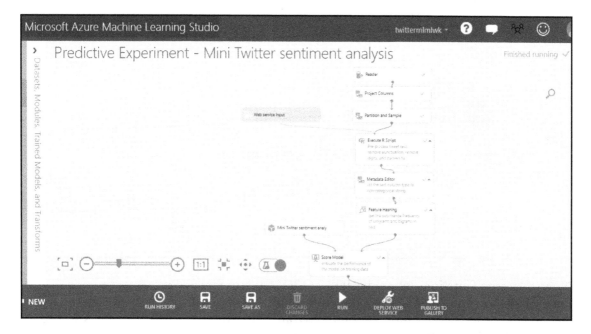

First, **Save** the experiment in your Azure ML workspace, then run it by clicking on the **Run** icon in the bottom menu bar. Once it has run successfully, click on **Deploy Web Service** and select **Deploy Web Service [Classic]**. A predictive experiment for your Twitter sentiment analysis will be created. In the **DASHBOARD** section, select the apps (**Excel 2010 or earlier notebook**) under **Default Endpoint**, which contains the experiment **API key**, **Web Service URL**, and **experiment** schema. Keep these credentials safe as these are needed for integrating the sentiment analysis web service model with Stream Analytics functions. Azure Blob storage can be optionally utilized here as reference data for storing unparsed discarded streams:

Now, select the **Functions** tab under **JOB TOPOLOGY** in Stream Analytics, provide the details like **Function Alias** & select **Function Type** as **Azure ML** and then add the credentials of the Twitter sentiment predictive analytics web service by clicking **Add** and selecting the appropriate machine learning model. You can use the same Azure subscription or just add the ML web service credentials (**URL**, **API Key**, and so on) manually. Then, update the **FUNCTION SIGNATURE**. Click on **Save** once you finish the integration of the Sentiment Analytics ML function with the Stream Analytics job:

The **FUNCTION SIGNATURE** code is defined as follows:

```
sentiment ( tweet_text NVARCHAR(MAX) ) RETURNS RECORD
```

> Detailed steps of integrating Azure Machine Learning function with Stream Analytics job is already covered in chapter 8 of this book.

Power BI can be chosen as the output of the Stream Analytics job. It gives real-time, interactive visualizations and analyzes tweet sentiments for the selected hashtags with the average positive, negative, and neutral sentiment scores. Add Power BI as the output of the Stream Analytics job and write the ASA job query as follows:

```
SELECT timestamp, topic, Result.[Score] as score, Result.[Sentiment] as
sentiment, text, id,
retweet_count, time_zone, lang INTO [PowerBIOutput] FROM
(SELECT DATEADD(ms, timestamp_ms, '1970-01-01') as timestamp,
Topic as topic, sentiment(text) as Result, Text, id, retweet_count,
time_zone, lang
FROM [TwitterStream]) TwitterStream;
```

While integrating Power BI as the output connector for the Stream Analytics job, the Power BI workspace, dataset, and table details need to be provided. Check `Chapter 4`, *Developing Real-Time Event Processing with Azure Streaming* of this book to learn more regarding integration of a Power BI as the output connector of a Stream Analytics job:

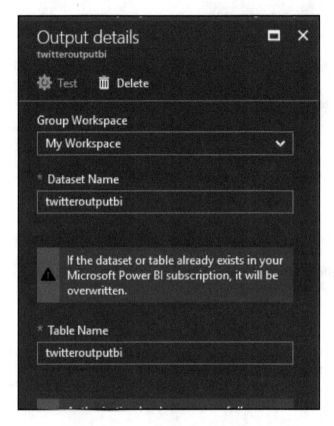

After the configuration is complete, finally, start the Stream Analytics Twitter Sentiment Analysis job. The output should be visible under the dataset of Power BI, along with the provided name and absolutely stunning, interactive, predictive analytics. The Twitter sentiment analytics predictive model can be built using the Power BI dashboard.

We can add visuals such as real-time total tweet count, topic-wise sentiment distribution by percentage, a word-cloud of the top tweet words with the maximum percentage of positive sentiments, count of tweet distributions by topic, average sentiment score by tweet language on the selected hashtags, and so on:

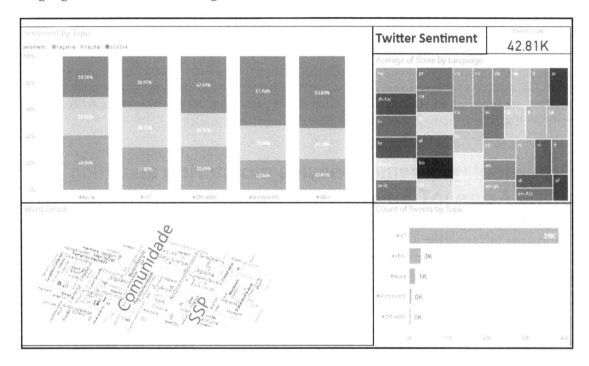

This entire solution for Twitter sentiment analytics can be integrated with Azure Functions by way of the app service model, and with different, assimilated operations through function events and webhooks. For example, from Twitter streaming to stream processing into Event Hubs, then processing the tweet events using a Stream Analytics job, integrating the Azure ML sentiment analytics web service, and finally pushing the output to a Power BI workspace dashboard.

Remote monitoring analytics using Azure IoT Suite

Azure IoT Suite is the one-stop shop for assisting your business with quick implementation of an IoT-based proof-of-concept, including preliminary solution architecture and solution of the project. The Suite configures the end-to-end architectural components using data simulation, ingestion, and processing along with real-time visualization layers. Even the solutions provide better visibility, by injecting your own devices, assets, and sensors located virtually, as well as managing collections with real-time device data using a remote monitoring **Proof of Concept** (**POC**), which sends automated alerts, triggering actions from remote diagnostics management to build device telemetry analytics.

Provisioning of remote device monitoring analytics using Azure IoT Suite

By provisioning remote monitoring telemetry analytics solutions, real-time sensors/smart devices can be connected with monitoring solutions to produce interactive alarms and analyze unstructured/semi-structured data that integrates business modules and improves automated solutions through Azure IoT Hub, Stream Analytics, Reference Data storage, Event Hubs, Azure WebJobs event processor hosts, and finally, visualization through Azure Web App smart device telemetry dashboards:

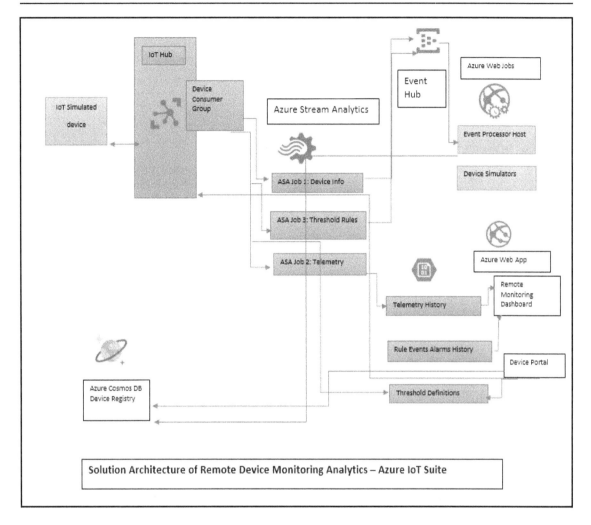

Solution Architecture of Remote Device Monitoring Analytics – Azure IoT Suite

In order to provision remote monitoring analytics, visit: `https://www.azureiotsuite.com`.

1. Login to Azure IoT Suite portal using your Azure account and then under **Provisioned solutions**, select **Create New Solution**. You may configure an appropriate Azure subscription directory if your Azure account is associated with multiple subscriptions:

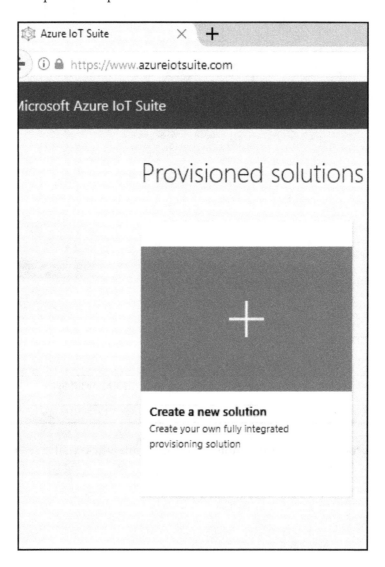

2. Choose **Remote Monitoring** as the solution type and click on **Select** to start provisioning the remote device telemetry use case PoC:

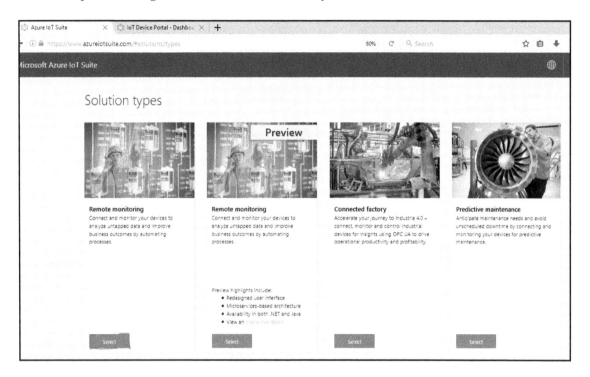

3. Next, provide your IoT analytics case study details by sharing the **Solution name**, **Subscription**, and **Region**. The solution name uniqueness will be checked during provisioning time itself. This solution uses one **IoT Hub**, one **Azure Active Directory app**, one **CosmosDB** account, two **Event Hubs**, one **Blob storage account** as reference data, three **Stream Analytics** jobs, each for device information, threshold parameters, and telemetry analytics, one **Azure Web App**, and **Web jobs** acting as event processors and a scheduler.

4. By clicking **Accept** on choosing your Azure subscription, authorize the solution to provide a Bing static map, specifying the remote location of the devices. Finally, click on the **Create Solution** button to provision the remote telemetry use case:

5. It'll take a few minutes to provision the entire solution, but once it's ready, you will be prompted to open the visual dashboard for the remote device monitoring analytics powered by the Azure Web App. You may track the provisioning status in real-time in the IoT Suite portal by clicking on the **Details** tab beneath the remote monitoring solution:

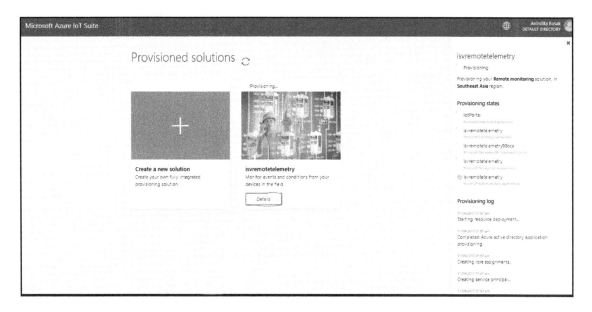

6. Now, once your remote monitoring device telemetry solution is ready in Azure IoT Suite, click on **Solution dashboard** to open the analytics dashboard. Optionally, you may also click on the **Launch** button to visualize the remote monitoring telemetry Azure Web App dashboard:

 You may have to sign in once more to authorize the remote monitoring analytics dashboard in Azure IoT Suite, authenticating through the Azure AD application.

The **Remote Monitoring Solution** dashboard consists of multiple, virtual weather sensors, including smart alarms/devices to monitor the status of weather temperature and minimum/maximum average device humidity over the last 24 hours by way of interactive graphs. The Bing map live visuals demonstrate device locations in various cities such as Seattle, Bellevue, Redmond, and so on.

Simultaneously, a new sensor can be integrated with a remote predictive telemetry analytics model, and alarms can be triggered by the device to an Azure IoT solution, and from IoT, monitoring the solution at the sensors level. The device monitoring telemetry history visual is parameterized and the appropriate temperature and humidity level can be analyzed by selecting the particular **coolingdevice-samples** for the device from a drop-down menu:

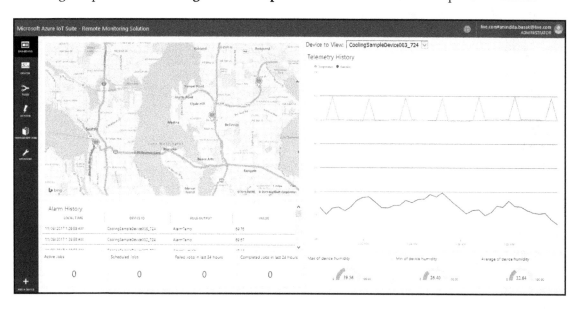

In order to integrate a new device with a remote monitoring solution, click on the Add **A Device** option in the lower-left menu and select **Add New** from the simulated virtual devices. If you have a physical hardware weather sensor, you may register it with the remote monitoring predictive analytics solution. You may generate a default **DeviceID** (case-sensitive), or can define your own DeviceID and click on **Create**.

If your device's cellular connectivity API is already registered with the IoT solution from the **API registration** section, then you may optionally select the **Attach a SIM ICCID to the device** checkbox:

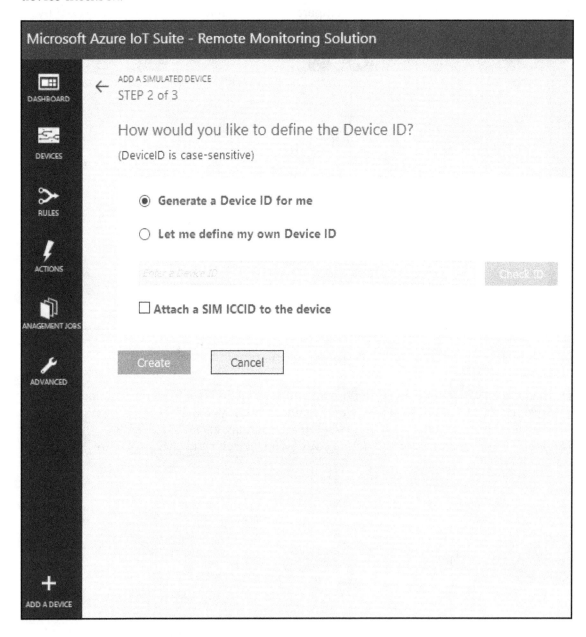

Next, a simulated IoT Hub Device ID will be registered with the remote monitoring solution app with **Device ID**, **IoT Hub hostname**, and **Device key details**. Click on **Done** to finish integrating the new device. The available devices registered with the monitoring solution are visible under the **Devices** tab, while the configured rules for temperature and humidity threshold values for each specific sensor are defined in the **Rules** section. The temperature/humidity level threshold parameters are editable under the **Edit Rules** option:

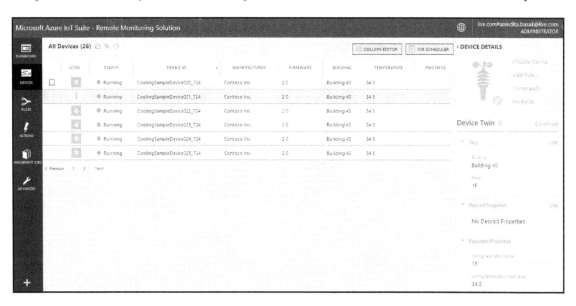

The **Actions** tab mainly defines **Action ID** indexes as alarms triggered from sensors, or sending messages through devices to the cloud, whereas the **Advanced** section specifies the smart-devices cellular API registration process with integration through an **API provider** (for example, Jasper or Ericsson), **device base Url, user credentials**, and so on:

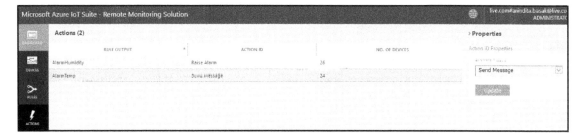

Now, if you check the Azure portal with the remote monitoring solution deployment name as the resource group, the resources deployed by remote monitoring will be visible. There will be three Stream Analytics jobs:

- **Device Info**: Analyzing device-based info-DeviceDataStream
- **Rules**: Analyzing the data streams from the device and device rules, mapped to temperature and humidity parameters
- **Telemetry**: Contains device-specific parameter statistics—temperature, humidity, and external temperature:

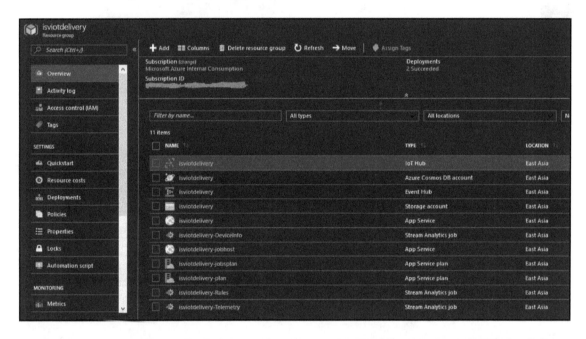

The latest preview version of the remote monitoring solution is also available and includes a redesigned device telemetry monitoring dashboard with global locations. It uses microservice-based, service-fabric-oriented architecture, and is available for both .NET and Java platforms. The deployment option is provided for both the basic (development) level and standard tier (production-ready), including high availability and scalability.

To learn more about harnessing the potential of remote monitoring telemetry with IoT, getting started with your digital transformation journey, utilizing your assets to get insights from your data, defining business protocols, and operationalizing values, visit this blog about Azure IoT Suite:
`https://cloud-platform-assets.azurewebsites.net/remote-monitoring/`
`Real-world case studies—There are multiple interesting real-life case studies available on Azure IoT remote monitoring solutions from Microsoft Customers: https://www.microsoft.com/en-us/internet-of-things/remote-monitoring`

Implementation of a connected factory use case using Azure IoT Suite

The connected factory use case is Microsoft's solution for helping an organization begin its journey with Industrie 4.0. Azure IoT Suite provides case study solutions for end-to-end, cloud-enabled industrial equipment, and deployed machines without disruption in the operation of device telemetry and data management, as well as the ability to predict possible failures in production lines. The connected factory solution in Azure IoT Suite is secure by design and verified with **OPC UA** components as developed from real-world **OPC UA** solutions. This use case easily extends to real-world factories by sustaining operations with preconfigured solutions.

OPC UA is the free cross-platform **machine to machine (M2M)** communication protocol built for industrial IoT automation implemented by OPC Foundation. To learn more click on `https://www.unified-automation.com/products.html`

Connected factory solution with Azure IoT Suite

The connected factory solution comes with six strategic introductory steps, as follows.

1. Determination of requirements for your asset digitization
2. Mock-up experiments with various data sources
3. Connecting various machines with OPC proxies and gateways
4. Building connected architectural pipelines and visualizations
5. Implementing operational data differences
6. Utilizing new, improved quality with scale

The solution architecture for a connected factory solution in Azure IoT Suite is shown as follows:

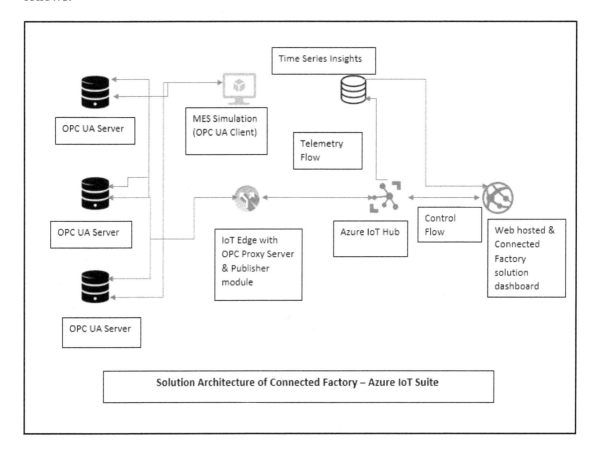

Solution Architecture of Connected Factory – Azure IoT Suite

The connected factory solution can be provisioned with the Azure IoT Suite portal by providing details such as **Solution name**, **Subscription**, and **Region**, and utilizing Azure resources such as the storage account (standard-LRS), Azure VM, time-series, the IoT Hub, Key Vault, and the Azure Web App.

On completion of **Connected factory** solution provisioning, click on the **Launch** button to open the dashboard. The factory location will be displayed on the left, along with the current and predicted alerts from various equipment. The visuals on overall equipment efficiency define overall efficiency, high availability, performance, and quality along with key performance indicator gauges of the factories. Click on any visual, such as machine efficiency from the last day and hour in Azure Time Series Insights:

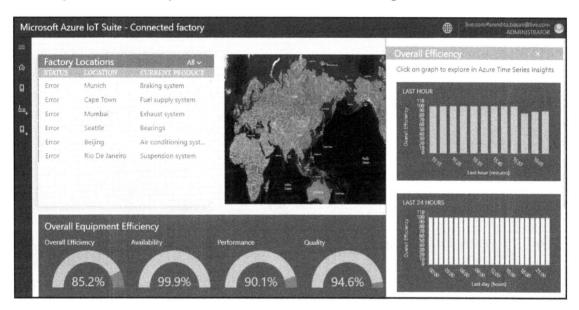

On selecting any equipment efficiency statistic, a time-series graph will load the detailed time-series events split by a device or application and its **unified resource identifier** (**URI**)/event source:

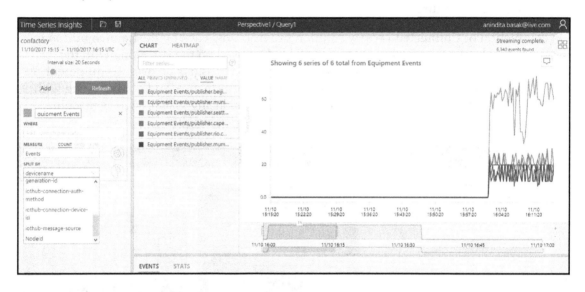

On selecting a particular factory line from a location, the current equipment production series (for example, brake pads) and suspected faults, execution, test, and assembly stages will be seen:

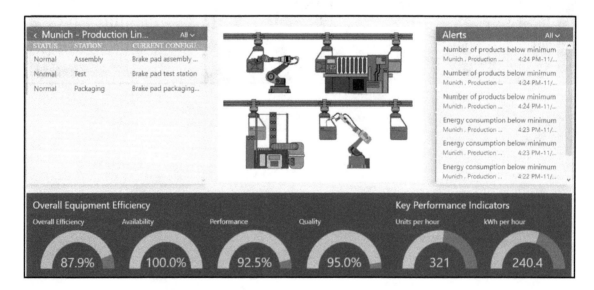

On further drilling down into equipment, the brake pad assembly shows the number of manufactured products over the last hour, faulty time comparison, energy cycle time, and so on, in Azure Time Series Insights visuals:

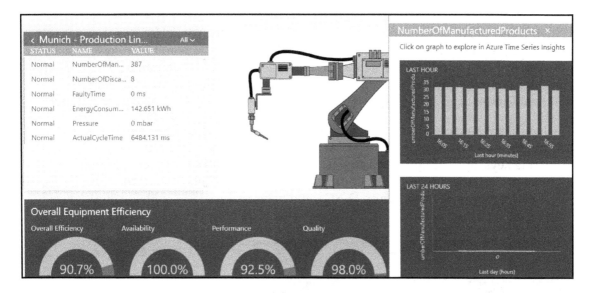

The Time Series Insights graph for **Azure IoT - Connected factory** shows events by display name and IoT Hub auth streams with devices, and looks as follows:

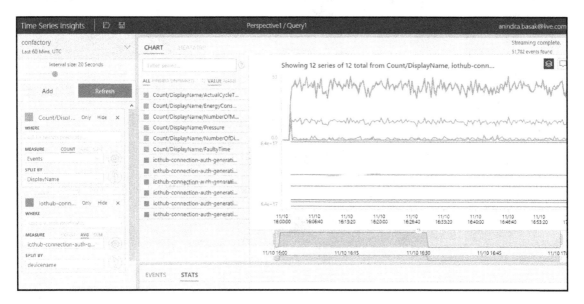

An Azure connected factory proof-of-concept solution contains resources by ingesting streams from OPC UA server complex modules to IoT Hub, from edge gateways to Azure Time Series Insights event sources, and the app service solution dashboard transforming operational data into actionable insights.

With the help of Azure IoT Suite preconfigured solutions, the connected factory use case provides better insights into production line assets for connection and monitoring, analysis of streams of data from equipment, machine-to-machine (M2M) communication, predicting possible failures by triggering alarms, and operationalizing full productivity and sustainable growth leveraging the four pillars of IoT—internet, data, people, and things.

The logical architecture of a connected factory consists of devices, edge gateways, which include **Trusted Platform Modules** (TPM) from OPC UA equipment to securely connect authoring keys, app configuration strings, passwords, and utilize a secure platform to authenticate each device and prevent unauthorized attacks. This is managed through Azure Key Vault, **network security group** (NSG), and network interfaces with a secure Azure VPN channel (virtual network):

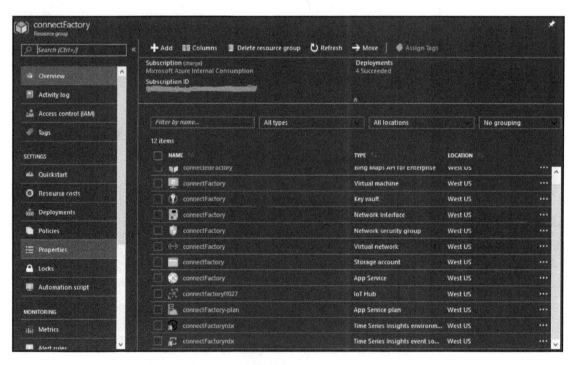

There is a preconfigured code solution available for a connected factory on GitHub at `https://github.com/Azure/azure-iot-connected-factory`

Real-world telecom fraud detection analytics using Azure Stream Analytics and Cortana Intelligence Gallery with interactive visuals from Microsoft Power BI

Each year, a billion-dollar business hits the news because of fraud, and this affects around one-third of global businesses, including telecom, insurance, financial, banking, and even retail. By its nature, fraud detection requires the significant procedure of intelligent data analytics to build prevention measures with the help of big data analytics, machine learning, smart artificial intelligence algorithms, and statistical measures in the cloud.

Implementation steps of fraud detection analytics using Azure Stream Analytics

In the telecom sector, a major issue is the detection of fraudulent incoming calls. This causes customers to get rid of unwanted, spam phone numbers. SIM card fraud analytics uses multiple call records originating from an identical source, but from different geographies, at the same time.

This requires strong **call detail record** (**CDR**) identification design patterns for a corresponding analysis pipeline:

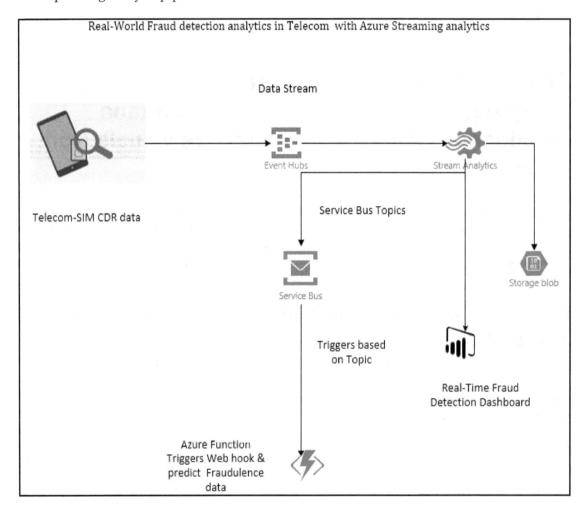

Solution Architecture of SIM card fraud detection analytics using Azure Stream Analytics

Prerequisites required for implementation of the Telco Fraud Detection Analytics using Azure Stream Analytics are:

- A valid Azure subscription
- Power BI Office 365 account
- Visual Studio

Steps for building the fraud detection analytics solution

The real-life implementation steps of SIM card fraud detection analytics using the Azure real-time data platform involves data ingestion, analysis, and visualization layers.

In order to get started with the generation of dummy **call details records** (**CDR**) data for simulation, perform the following:

1. First, we need to build up the `TelcoDataGeneratorDemo` solution in Visual Studio as a **C#.NET console** app, with classes such as `CallStore` (for generating a random number of calls from countries and processing them in a loop), `CDRecord` (defines the CDR data parameters by setting up proper CDR format), `GenConfig` (for designing the output CDR data in a format of sets, fileDump, %CallBackRatio, and so on), and finally, a program file for the generation of raw dummy data. In your `program.cs` define methods, such as `GenerateFraudCallData`, add the following code:

```
// Generate data
 static void GenerateFraudCallData(string[] args)
 {
 Queue callBackQ = new Queue();
// Parse parameters
 // Number of cdr records, probability of fraud, and number of
hours
 GenConfig config = new GenConfig(Int32.Parse(args[0]),
float.Parse(args[1]), Int32.Parse(args[2]));
// print statistics
 Console.Error.WriteLine(config);
// Start the generation
// Generate the call nos
 CallStore FraudmobileNos = new CallStore(100000);
int numCallbackPerFile = (int) (config.nCallBackPercent *
config.nCDRPerFile);
```

2. Next, you need to design the CDR data generation per call set and then update the call numbers with the number of hours:

```
// Start generating per set
 DateTime simulationTime = DateTime.Now;
 Random r = new Random();
bool invalidRec = false;
 bool genCallback = false;
// TOOD: Update this to number of hours
 DateTimeOffset ptTime = DateTimeOffset.Now;
 DateTimeOffset endTime = ptTime.AddHours(config.nDurationHours);
   while ( endTime.Subtract(ptTime) >= TimeSpan.Zero )
```

```
{
DateTimeOffset currentTime = ptTime;
Console.WriteLine(String.Format("{0:yyyyMMdd HHmmss}",
simulationTime));
```

3. Now, design a few loops in the `GenerateFraudCallData` method and identify whether to generate an invalid call record or not. There will be a callback associated with data, to determine calling and called spam phone numbers, and call duration:

```
for (int cdr = 0; cdr < config.nCDRPerFile; cdr++)
{
currentTime = ptTime;
// Determine whether to generate an invalid CDR record
double presentValue = r.NextDouble();
if (presentValue < 0.1)
invalidRec = true;
else
invalidRec = false;
// Determine whether there will be a callback
presentValue = r.NextDouble();
if (presentValue >= config.nCallBackPercent)
genCallback = true;
else
genCallback = false;
// Determine called and calling num
int calledIdx = r.Next(0, FraudmobileNos.CallNos.Length);
int callingIdx = r.Next(0, FraudmobileNos.CallNos.Length);
CDRrecord recCDR = new CDRrecord();
recCDR.setData("FileNum", "" + cdr);
int switchIdx = r.Next(0, FraudmobileNos.switchCountries.Length);
int switchAltIdx = r.Next(0,
FraudmobileNos.switchCountries.Length);
// Find an alternate switch
while (switchAltIdx == switchIdx)
{
switchAltIdx = r.Next(0, FraudmobileNos.switchCountries.Length);
}
recCDR.setData("SwitchNum",
FraudmobileNos.switchCountries[switchIdx]);
```

4. You can also check the code to see whether an invalid call record exists or not, and then set the data with `Date`, `Time`, `CallingPhoneNumber`, and `CalledPhoneNumber` schemas:

```
if (invalidRec)
{
```

```
recCDR.setData("Date", "F");
recCDR.setData("Time", "F");
recCDR.setData("DateTime", "F F");
}
else
{
String callDate = String.Format("{0:yyyyMMdd}", currentTime);
String callTime = String.Format("{0:HHmmss}", currentTime);
recCDR.setData("Date", callDate);
recCDR.setData("Time", callTime);
recCDR.setData("DateTime", callDate + " " + callTime);
String calledNum = FraudmobileNos.CallNos[calledIdx];
String callingNum = FraudmobileNos.CallNos[callingIdx];
recCDR.setData("CalledNum", calledNum);
recCDR.setData("CallingNum", callingNum);
```

5. Finally, SIM card fraud detection records can be generated, integrating numbers with various schemas from the CDR dataset with call duration, and then enqueue it:

```
// Sim card fraud record
if (genCallback)
{
// For call back the A->B end has duration 0
recCDR.setData("CallPeriod", "0");
// need to generate another set of no
calledIdx = callingIdx;
callingIdx = r.Next(0, FraudmobileNos.CallNos.Length);
CDRrecord callbackRec = new CDRrecord();
callbackRec.setData("FileNum", "" + cdr);
callbackRec.setData("SwitchNum",
FraudmobileNos.switchCountries[switchAltIdx]);
//callbackRec.setData("SwitchNum", "" + (f + 1));
// Pertub second
int pertubs = r.Next(0, 30);
callDate = String.Format("{0:yyyyMMdd}", currentTime);
callTime = String.Format("{0:HHmmss}",
currentTime.AddMinutes(pertubs));
callbackRec.setData("Date", callDate);
callbackRec.setData("Time", callTime);
callbackRec.setData("DateTime", callDate + " " + callTime);
// Set it as the same calling IMSI
callbackRec.setData("CallingIMSI", recCDR.CDRCallingIMSI);
calledNum = FraudmobileNos.CallNos[calledIdx];
callingNum = FraudmobileNos.CallNos[callingIdx];
callbackRec.setData("CalledNum", calledNum);
callbackRec.setData("CallingNum", callingNum);
// Determine duration of call
```

```
        int callPeriod = r.Next(1, 1000);
        callbackRec.setData("CallPeriod", "" + callPeriod);
       // Enqueue the call back rec
        callBackQ.Enqueue(callbackRec);
        cdr++;
        }
        else
        {
        int callPeriod = r.Next(1, 800);
        recCDR.setData("CallPeriod", "" + callPeriod);
        }
        }
```

After enqueuing, data could be put in a queue for processing and storing. As defined in the solution architecture, this CDR dummy data would be ingested directly into Azure Service Bus Event Hubs. So, before generating CDR data, make sure the Service Bus Event Hub is provisioned and take a note of its connection string since it will be used in this TelcoDataGenerator C# simulator app:

The last phase of code for the GenerateFraudCallData method is as follows:

```
 // send cdr rec to output
 //if (genCallback) Console.Write("callback A->B ");
 outputCDRRecs(recCDR);
 if (callBackQ.Count > 0 andand (cdr % 7 == 0))
 {
 CDRrecord drec;
 drec = (CDRrecord)callBackQ.Dequeue();
 outputCDRRecs(drec);
 //Console.Write("callback C->A!");
 //outputCDRRecs(s, f, drec);
 }
 // Sleep for 1000ms
 System.Threading.Thread.Sleep(100);
 // get the current time after generation
 ptTime = DateTimeOffset.Now;
 } // cdr
 // Clear the remaining entries in the call back queue
 if (callBackQ.Count > 0)
 {
 // need to empty queue
 while (callBackQ.Count > 0)
 {
 CDRrecord dr = (CDRrecord)callBackQ.Dequeue();
 outputCDRRecs(dr);
 //outputCDRRecs(s, f, dr);
 }
```

```
    }
// close the file
  if (writer != null)
  {
writer.Flush();
writer.Close();
  writer = null;
  }
```

The major attributes of CDR for fraudulent phone records are as follows:

- **CallrecTime**: Call start time timestamp value
- **SwitchNum**: The phone switch connecting the call representing different countries
- **CallingNum**: The caller phone number
- **CallingMSI**: **International Mobile Subscriber Identity** (**IMSI**) is the number defining the originating caller's identity
- **CalledNum**: The recipient phone number
- **CalledMSI**: IMSI identifier of the called number

The complete sample code for the TelcoData generator C# simulator app is available with the code section of this book.

Next, the Stream Analytics job should be created for analyzing the ingested CDR data and integrating input with Event Hubs, processing fraudulent call records, transforming the stream records with the total count, applying joining to identify if it is the same caller or not, indicated by IMSI, and incoming call duration differences using an ASA-SQL query:

```
SELECT System.Timestamp AS WindowEnd, COUNT(*) AS FraudulentCalls
INTO "CallRecordStream-PowerBI"
FROM "CallRecordStream" CS1 TIMESTAMP BY CallRecTime
JOIN "CallRecordStream" CS2 TIMESTAMP BY CallRecTime
/* Where the caller is the same, as indicated by IMSI (International Mobile
Subscriber Identity) */
ON CS1.CallingIMSI = CS2.CallingIMSI
/* ...and date between CS1 and CS2 is between one and five seconds */
AND DATEDIFF(ss, CS1, CS2) BETWEEN 1 AND 5
/* Where the switch location is different */
WHERE CS1.SwitchNum != CS2.SwitchNum
GROUP BY TumblingWindow(Duration(second, 1))
```

The output layer could be associated with Power BI for a quick visualization of total fraudulent calls originating from the same number and region, call analysis by time-series window, and so on:

Alternatively, the processed fraudulent call records output could be analyzed through Service Bus topics integrated with the fraud detection Stream Analytics job and stored in Azure Redis Cache, which could then be stored in an Azure SQL DB based on Function app webhook events. The code snippet for the Fraud Detection Function app looks as follows:

```
using System;
using System.Threading.Tasks;
using StackExchange.Redis;
using Newtonsoft.Json;
using System.Configuration;
public static void Run(string sbQueueItem, TraceWriter log)
{
log.Info($"Function processed through Service Bus Queue message:
{sbQueueItem}");
// Connection refers to a property that returns a ConnectionMultiplexer
IDatabase db = Connection.GetDatabase();
log.Info($"Created database {db}");
// Parse JSON and extract the time
var message = JsonConvert.DeserializeObject<dynamic>(sbQueueItem);
string time = message.time;
string callingnum1 = message.callingnum1;
// Perform cache operations using the cache object for putting call records
in key/value pair...
// Simple put of integral data types into the cache
string key = time + " - " + callingnum1;
db.StringSet(key, sbQueueItem);
```

```
log.Info($"Object put in database. Key is {key} and value is
{sbQueueItem}");
// Simple get of data types from the cache
string value = db.StringGet(key);
log.Info($"Database got: {value}");
}
// Connect to the Service Bus
private static Lazy<ConnectionMultiplexer> lazyConnection = new
Lazy<ConnectionMultiplexer>(() =>
{
return ConnectionMultiplexer.Connect("<<Your Azure Redis Cache Connection
String");
});
public static ConnectionMultiplexer Connection
{
get
{
return lazyConnection.Value;
}
}
```

The final, transformed data consists of metadata evaluating real-time fraudulent calls around the globe with quick visuals in Power BI, storage in Blob storage for further analysis, processing through webhook events with Function apps from Redis Cache, and enqueued messages through a Service Bus topic from the Stream Analytics job.

You can also test the query of a fraud detection Stream Analytics job by clicking on the icon bubbles beside the CallStream Event Hub input connector, and select the **Sample data from input** option:

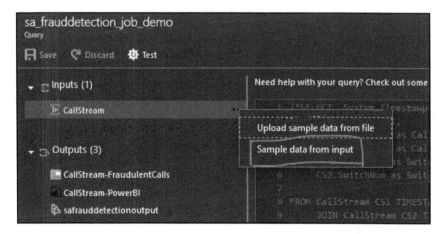

Keep the duration at the default 3 minutes and click **OK** to upload the sampled input from the Stream Analytics job:

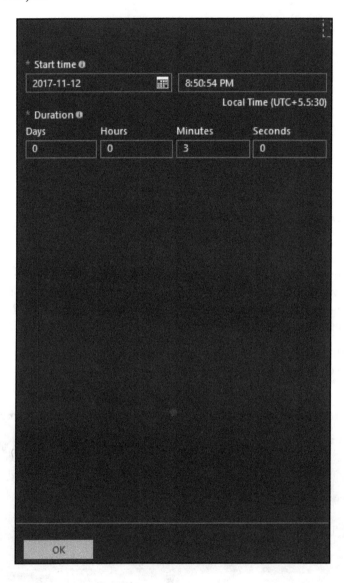

Using the **Test** button in the upper-left menu of the job portal, we can generate the query output with the sample input data.

The final output results in the count of total fraudulent calls by timestamp and looks as follows:

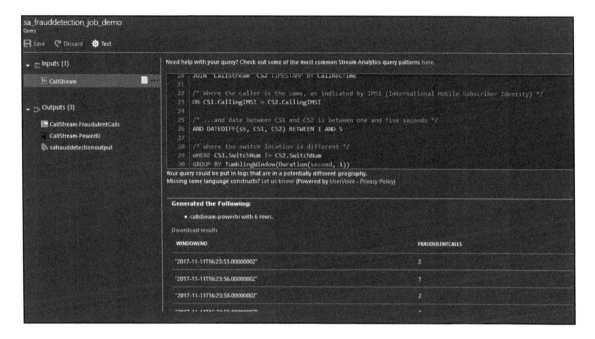

To learn more, the complete use case solution for the real-world, Telco Fraud Detection Analysis with Azure Stream Analytics is available in Cortana Intelligence Gallery at `https://gallery.cortanaintelligence.com/Tutorial/Using-Azure-Stream-Analytics-for-Real-time-fraud-detection-2`

Summary

In this chapter, we have introduced building real-world case studies involving Stream Analytics as a component of the Azure real-time data analytics platform by engaging in step-by-step guidance and demonstrating a real-life proof-of-concept: social sentiment analytics utilizing a Twitter live feed and smart Azure supervised machine learning models.

We also had an evaluation of Azure IoT Suite as a preconfigured business solution, specifying domains such as remote device telemetry monitoring using Stream Analytics with Azure data stack, building up solutions for a connected factory, and implementation steps of real-life SIM card fraud detection analytics with Azure Stream Analytics and the PaaS (Platform as a Service) environment.

Index